Investing FOR DUMMIES®

PORTABLE EDITION

by Tony Levene

WILEY

A John Wiley and Sons, Ltd, Publication

Investing For Dummies®, Portable Edition

Published by
John Wiley & Sons, Ltd
The Atrium
Southern Gate
Chichester
West Sussex
PO19 8SQ
England

E-mail (for orders and customer service enquires): cs-books@wiley.co.uk

Visit our Home Page on www.wiley.com

For general information on our other products and services, please contact our Customer Care Department within the U.S. at 877-762-2974, outside the U.S. at 317-572-3993, or fax 317-572-4002.

For technical support, please visit www.wiley.com/techsupport.

Wiley also publishes its books in a variety of electronic formats. Some content that appears in print may not be available in electronic books.

British Library Cataloguing in Publication Data: A catalogue record for this book is available from the British Library

ISBN 978-1-119-97434-5 (paperback), ISBN 978-1-119-97466-6 (ebk),

ISBN 978-1-119-97467-3 (ebk), ISBN 978-1-119-97468-0 (ebk)

Printed and bound in Great Britain by CPI Antony Rowe, Chippenham, Wiltshire.

10 9 8 7 6 5 4 3 2 1

WILEY

About the Author

Tony Levene has been a journalist for some 35 years after a brief career teaching French. He writes on issues ranging from investment to consumer rights. Over his career, he has worked for newspapers including *The Guardian, The Sunday Times, Sunday Express, Daily Express, The Sun, Daily Star* and *Sunday Mirror*. He has also published eight previous books on investment and financial issues. He lives in London with his wife Claudia, and cats Plato, Pandora and Pascal. He has 'two grown-up' children, Zoë and Oliver.

Dedication

This book is dedicated to Claudia, for her patience during the book's gestation; to Oliver for persuading me to write it; and to Zoë for her suggestions and approval of my initial chapter. I would also like to thank my brother Stuart for giving me sanctuary away from phones and other distractions whilst I wrote much of it.

Author's Acknowledgements

I would like to thank Daniel Mersey and Steve Edwards at Wiley for their patience and help during the various stages of this book. And an especial thank you to Sandra Lynn Blackthorn (Sandy), for all her work in turning my manuscript from a book about investment into *Investing For Dummies*. I am also grateful for the forebearance of my Guardian colleagues every time I mentioned 'the book'.

But most of all, I would like to acknowledge Peter Shearlock. Peter, whom I first met at school when we were both aged 11, was responsible for starting my career as an investment writer and has helped me invaluably along the way. He gave me my first lessons in the irrationality that often characterises financial markets and introduced me to 'City characters' ranging from spivs and chancers to the epitome of blue-blooded respectability. It is this variety that makes investing so fascinating. Thanks, Peter.

Publisher's Acknowledgements

We're proud of this book; please send us your comments through our Dummies online registration form located at www.dummies.com/register/.

Some of the people who helped bring this book to market include the following:

Commissioning, Editorial, and Media Development

Project Editor: Steve Edwards

Content Editor: Jo Theedom

Commissioning Editor: David Palmer

Assistant Editor: Ben Kemble

Copy Editor: Charlie Wilson

Technical Editor: Julian Knight

Proofreader: Jamie Brind

Production Manager: Daniel Mersey

Cover Photos: © First Light/Alamy

Cartoons: Ed McLachlan

Composition Services

Project Coordinator: Kristie Rees

Layout and Graphics: Melanee Habig

Proofreader: Jessica Kramer

Indexer: Potomac Indexing, LLC

Contents at a Glance

Contents

Introduction

So much has happened for investors in almost the twinkling of an eye, it's certainly time for a new edition of *Investing For Dummies*.

You'd have to be around 100 years old to remember the last time the world was so convulsed by economic and investment markets crises.

Over the past couple of years we've watched a run on a small UK bank, the forced nationalisation of two more, the collapse of some of New York's biggest investment banks, mayhem in the US housing finance market, the bankruptcy of Icelandic banks, the rescue of the Greek and many other smaller European economies in the eurozone, record low interest rates almost everywhere guaranteeing that savers get a bad deal, and the rise of economies such as India and China – and that's only scratching at the surface of all the recent changes in the world of investing.

On top of all that's happened in the big bad world, understanding investment has become more crucial than ever thanks to the end of so many guaranteed pensions from employers. Knowing about investments could almost have been a hobby when I wrote the first edition of *Investing For Dummies* nearly a decade ago. Now, you're out there on your own with pension investment decisions.

But not everything has changed in the investment world. No matter how chaotic it may seem, or how complex the hedge fund universe appears to all but those with a double degree in investment rocket science, the essentials remain the same.

Investment markets are still a battleground between fear and greed. How else to explain one set of investors bailing out a country's failing economy only to be replaced with others who hope to profit from what's left?

And neither *Investing For Dummies* nor any other source of advice will ever be right all the time. If you can get more than half of your decisions right and beat the averages, then you're doing as well as you're likely to. This applies to the so-called experts and professionals as well.

This book gives you the facts upfront and honestly. So you'll find no magic formula for wealth here. Besides, even if there were a get-rich-quick recipe, I wouldn't be telling anyone about it; I'd be using it.

No one can predict which shares will do well (although that doesn't seem to stop people from asking me for sure-fire tips at parties). But what I can provide is guidance to help you make sensible decisions that suit your circumstances.

Investing involves more than understanding an economics textbook or balance sheet. It involves understanding a whole lot about human reactions to the ups and downs of money, plus (really important) understanding how you react. And it's fascinating because it's where you find all the drama of human life, because investment values represent nothing other than the combination of the minds of all the people involved in investment markets.

Over the three decades and more that I've been writing about money, I've continued to find investing a fascinating subject and endeavour, and I've become moderately more well off than I would've otherwise been. I hope that this book helps you become fascinated with investing too. And I also hope that by reading it, you'll be better off than you would've otherwise been.

About This Book

This book is designed to be read in several ways. It's a reference book, so you don't have to read the chapters in chronological order, from front to back, although of course you can read it cover to cover, like a novel, to gain appreciation for the huge variety of investment opportunities that are available. (If you approach the book this way, I suggest doing so with pen and paper at the ready so that you can note areas for further research on the Internet or from publications such as the *Financial Times.*) Or you can just pick a topic that interests you or go straight to a section that answers a particular question you have.

But my preferred way for you to read this book is to go through Part I and *then* pick up on the investments that concern or interest you. For example, after reading Part I you may want to go straight to Part III to find out what collective investments are because, say, an advert about collective investments has caught your eye or a financial adviser has suggested one or two of them. Likewise, you may want to skip the chapter on buy-to-let properties because, say, being a do-it-yourself landlord is the last thought on your mind.

Conventions Used in This Book

I've tried to avoid jargon as much as I can, but know that the investment world is full of it. Like all professions and occupations, finance and investment have their own insider language that's intended to mystify outsiders. When I do use the industry's language in the text, I *italicise* the term and define it for you in an easy-to-understand way.

Foolish Assumptions

While writing this book, I made some assumptions about you:

- ✔ You're either completely new to investing or have limited information about it, and you want someone to help you understand what investing is really about and what types of investments are available.

- ✔ You don't want to become an expert investor at this point in your life. You just want the basics – in informal, easy-to-understand language.

- ✔ You want to make up your *own* mind while using a guide through the investment jungle. You want enough pointers for you to risk only what you can afford to lose and for you to make a worthwhile return on your hard-earned cash.

How This Book Is Organised

This book has five major parts, or themes. Each part is divided into chapters relating to the theme, and each chapter is subdivided into individual sections relating to the chapter's topic. In addition, to help you pinpoint your specific area of interest, I include a detailed Table of Contents at the beginning of the book and a detailed Index at the end.

Part 1: Investment Basics

This is an essential part for understanding investing in general. I take you through what investment means, explain how to assess what you already have and the sort of returns you can expect, offer some insight on specific emotions that make investors tick, talk about the idea of risk and reward, and get you into the habit of reading the small print in investment situations. Most importantly, though, this part enables you to find out a lot about yourself and how you may face up to finance.

Part 11: Shares and Bonds

In this part, I look at how financial markets operate and ways of analysing markets and companies. I explain what makes a market, examine the big companies and world markets, provide tips and titbits for when you begin investing in the stock market, cover what you need to know about stock-market-quoted companies, give you the scoop on investing in bonds and explain how to get pertinent information (because investment markets revolve around information).

Part 111: Collective Investments

This part is where you find out about ready-made investment products. I talk about unit trusts, investment trusts and hedge funds, explaining what they really are and how they work – to help you decide whether investing in them is right for you. And I let you in on the fact that you can actually perform as well as the average fund manager or stockbroker by throwing a dart at a shares price page that's pinned to your wall.

Part IV: Property and Alternatives

Many people no longer want to confine investment to trading pieces of paper such as stocks and shares. Instead, they aim to buy and sell real things that they hope will go up in value. So this part covers investing in property, from a second home for renting out to tenants to big commercial buildings. In addition, this part covers alternative investments. I'm not talking about fashioned alternative investments, like art and vintage cars, but investments based on things like stock, commodity and currency markets where you go nowhere near buying the shares, metals or foreign exchange contracts on which they're based. Be warned up front, though, that these alternatives are *not* for the faint of heart. Some are really only one step removed from the betting shop or casino. Risky, risky.

Part V: The Part of Tens

This part gives you a taste of *For Dummies* tradition. Every *For Dummies* book has this part, which always contains lists of tens. Here, I give you ten tips on how to find a good adviser and ten helpful hints to consider before investing that first penny.

Icons Used in This Book

I've highlighted some information in this book with icons:

This icon points out useful titbits or helpful advice on the topic at hand.

I use this icon to highlight important information that you'll want to keep in mind, so don't forget this stuff!

This icon points out just that – a warning – so take heed. The investment world is full of sharks and other nasties. I don't want you to lose your money to crummy schemes and criminals.

You'll find this icon next to, well, technical stuff that you may want to skip. I've been sparing with this stuff because investment can be pretty technical anyway. (Note that even though you may want to skip this material on your first reading, and please feel free to, this info may be worthwhile coming back to later with your greater knowledge of the fundamentals.)

Where to Go from Here

This book is set up so you can dive in wherever you want. Feel free to go straight to Chapter 1 and start reading from the beginning to the end. Or look through the Table of Contents, find your area of interest and flip right to that page. Or better yet, read Part I and *then* flip right to that page of interest. Your call.

Wherever you go from here, if you find a piece of advice or a warning that you think applies especially to you, copy it down and then fix it to the fridge with a magnet, or pin it on a board.

And as you read through this book, either in part or in whole, why not practise some dry-run investing? Buying a dummy portfolio using pretend money is always a good way of getting familiar with investment without the worry of losing money.

Part I
Investment Basics

In this part . . .

*T*he absolute basics. If that's what you need, then this part is where you'll find them.

Here, I tell you what the term *investment* really means and introduce you to five basic investment choices. In addition, I explain how to assess what you already have and the sort of returns you can expect. I get into a little bit of investor psychology too, letting you know some specific emotions that make investors tick. I also talk about risk and reward – the benefits and drawbacks of various investment possibilities and ways to increase your odds of successful returns. And I discuss the great importance of reading the small print in all investment situations. A lot of info, yes. But I present it in a friendly, easy-to-understand way, especially for beginner investors.

Chapter 1

Taking Your First Steps on the Money Trail

In This Chapter

▶ Understanding basic investment philosophy

▶ Discovering your own money make-up

▶ Looking at what you may be investing already

▶ Getting familiar with five basic investment choices

*T*his chapter explains the first steps to take in your investing ventures. But take heed: in this chapter (and throughout the book) you need to think deeply about some personal matters, to understand yourself, to know where you're going in your life and what makes you tick. In other words, you need to wear two hats – that of investor *and* that of philosopher. Be prepared for some tests that ask what sort of person you are, what you want for yourself and what you're prepared to do for it. If you don't see a test, that's no bar to testing yourself. The decisions you make are down to you alone.

Understanding the facts and mechanics of investment decisions is just a start. Knowing how to apply them to your own circumstances, and to those of your family and other dependants, is what will make your strategy succeed.

What's Your Reason for Investing?

This section is basic, comprised of just one simple *Investing For Dummies* test question: why did you buy this book? Chances are you probably did so for one of these four reasons:

✔ **You have no money but want to make some.** Most people fall into this category. You want to invest some money and accumulate funds but don't know where to start. How you go about it depends on how well you can discipline yourself. Take heart, though: even the most confirmed shopaholic can build up a nest-egg.

✔ **You have some money, want it to make more and currently make your own investment decisions.** You're the traditional investor who wants to make your personal wealth grow. You already make your own investment decisions and want to get better at it. How you go about it depends on who you are, how you made your money and where you hope to be in 5, 10 or 20 years.

✔ **You have some money, want it to make more and currently have others handle the investment process for you.** Maybe fund managers handle your investments so you can gain tax advantages or because your savings are lumped together with those of others in a pension or similar fund. Maybe your life is too busy or complicated for you to do the investing yourself. Regardless, you now want to understand how investing works so you can take over your own investment decisions or monitor what fund managers are doing with your cash. I'm not sure many people will pick up this book to check up on fund managers, but I could be wrong.

✔ **You're now in charge of your pension decisions.** Unless you work in the public sector, the chances are that you now have to take stock of your pension. What you get when you retire is now largely up to you rather than your former employer or employers.

What's Your Personality Type with Money?

Some people spend all they have each month (and then some on top – ouch!). Others put away a bit in the bank or building society on a regular basis. And still others buy and sell stocks and shares, with some going in for some very complex investments.

Test time: you need to decide whether you're a spender, a saver or an investor. Doing so isn't as easy, though. Spenders can be savers or investors. Savers can be spenders and investors. And investors are generally also savers and must, at some stage, be spenders. But most people are predominantly one of the three types – spender, saver or investor. Which category you think you fit into determines what you do from now on, how you react and how you progress.

Spenders have fun

Spenders are generally people who live for the here and now. They may want more than they can have and end up borrowing money, probably on plastic cards. For many spenders, accumulating cash for the future has no priority.

Here are ten attributes of spenders. If the majority of them apply to you, then, yep, you're a spender:

- You don't look forward to the end of the month.
- You love new things – the glossier the better.
- You have more than one credit card.
- You can't resist two-for-one offers.
- You buy unnecessary clothes.
- You're always first and last to buy a round of drinks.
- You believe in living a lot now.
- You see the future as a foreign land.
- You worry about money at times.
- You buy glossy magazines as much for the advertisements as the articles.

If you're in this category, your first priority is to recognise that investors can't always be spenders. Getting familiar with investing is a good way to accomplish this priority because it offers an alternative use for your cash.

Know that while on your way to becoming a saver or an investor, you can start with very small sums. You can become a saver with £1. And some regular stock-market based investment plans start at £20 a month, around the cost of a small packet of crisps a day.

Savers have cash

Savers are people who want to keep their financial cake and eat small slices at a later date. Here are ten saver attributes. Tick those that apply to you, and if the majority do, then you're probably a saver:

☐ You have a surplus at the end of each month.

☐ You go to the supermarket with a shopping list.

☐ You don't have a credit card, or you pay it off in full each month.

☐ You're prepared to put off purchases.

☐ You'd rather buy second-hand than run up a debt.

☐ Your property is more important than your furniture.

☐ You look at the display windows at banks and building societies.

☐ You know what the current interest rates are.

☐ You believe in the saying *waste not, want not.*

☐ You've read *Frugal Living For Dummies* (published by Wiley) – or, if you haven't, you'll get a copy the next time you book shop.

Saving is a stage you must reach before investing. You can be a saver as well as an investor, but you can't be an investor without first saving up some money to invest.

Investors build up future funds

Investors are people who are prepared to go the extra mile to try to ensure that their wealth goes the extra thousands, tens of thousands or even more. Investors want control over their money but are ready to take a risk provided that they're in charge and know the odds. They want their money to work hard for them – as hard as they worked to get the money.

You don't need an MBA, a posh old school tie or stacks of money. However, know that although you can sleepwalk into saving your cash, you must be wide awake to be an investor.

As a pure saver, you don't have to know what you're doing. You can just stash your cash under the bed, for example. As an investor, you *must* know what you're doing and have the self-discipline to follow your strategy, even if the strategy is doing nothing, buying and forgetting, or benign neglect.

So are you an investor? Check out these attributes to find out:

- You have spare cash.
- You have an emergency fund for the day the roof falls down or the car collapses.
- You want more than the bank or building society offers.
- You think about your money-making strategy and tactics.
- You can face up to bad days on investment markets without worry.
- You're ready to swap certitude for a bigger potential reward.
- You can afford to lock away your spare cash for five years at the very least.
- You understand what you're doing with your money.
- You're prepared to lose money occasionally.
- You're ready to invest your time into growing your fortune.

All of these attributes belong to an investor. So, what's your bottom-line personality type when it comes to money?

- **You decided you're an investor.** Congratulations! You're ready to embark on the road to growing your money. It won't be easy. You may face stiff climbs, vertiginous falls, rocky surfaces, long deviations and dead ends. But give it enough work and time, and I promise that investing will work out.
- **You didn't qualify as an investor.** You got as far as a saver and no further. Or you're really stuck as a spender. You're wishing you'd spent the price of this book on something else or stuck it in your savings account, where at current savings rates it will double in about 35 years.

Well, don't regret your purchase or vow to send this book off for recycling, or try to recoup some of the price by selling it. Stick with it. The fact that you bought this book shows you're ready to move on to investing when you're financially and psychologically ready.

Even if you decide you never want to buy a share, sell a bond, invest in a unit trust or check on foreign exchange rates, this book is still for you. Why? Because you're almost certainly an investor already. (The following section tells you how, if your curiosity is piqued.)

Surprise! You've Probably Been Investing Already

Your financial fate already depends on the ups and downs of the stocks and shares markets. Few people can escape this fact, and every day the number of people who can ignore the investment world diminishes. You may be an unconscious investor or even an unwilling one, but there's no running away from it; you're already an investor.

Investing through your pension fund

The biggest amount of investment money you're likely to have is the value of your pension fund. Whether you pay into it yourself, rely on your employer or build it up in partnership with your employer, it all rides on investment markets.

Just to give you an idea of how much you may have, suppose that you earn £25,000 a year and put 10 per cent of your earnings each month into a pension fund that grows at a 7 per cent average per year. Here's what your fund will be worth over the course of 45 years (I've ignored tax relief on pension contributions, future wage rises, inflation, and fund and pension management charges to keep this example simple):

Number of years	Value of fund
5	£14,915
10	£36,059
15	£66,032
20	£108,525
25	£168,762
30	£254,157
35	£375,214
40	£546,827
45	£790,111

That's serious money! And it all started with a first monthly payment of just £208! Of course, the assumptions I make are foolish. No one continues on a flat salary for 45 years – some see earnings soar and others stop work. And although the annual growth rate I've used is an average based on the past, whatever happens in the future, it won't be smooth!

Most people haven't a clue that they have the potential for anything like the preceding example over a working lifetime. But even if you're aware of what you could achieve, I bet you didn't know that you have a good chance of taking some investment control over that sum. Even if you don't want to, at least you should be able to check up on what the pension fund managers are doing with your money. Understanding what other people are doing with your money can help you increase your own pension fund in good markets and prevent it from going down when the investment world turns sour.

Note that your pension plan isn't the only area where you may be an unwitting stocks and shares investor. Endowment mortgages and other investment-linked insurance schemes also revolve around stocks and shares.

Investing through a share in your firm's fortunes

Millions of people are potential investors in the company they work for. Most big stock-market-quoted companies, like British Airways or Wal-Mart's UK offshoot Asda, offer employees option plans that give workers the chance to acquire a stake in the firm. To acquire that stake, workers buy *shares*, also known as *equities*, which are explained in the section 'Get your share of shares', later in this chapter.

The original idea was that giving someone the chance to buy shares in the future at a price fixed in the past would help motivate staff members and make them put in more effort, but in reality the idea only works if all colleagues work *equally* hard. The original idea aside, the option plan is just a pay perk, but one that can be valuable. A variety of schemes are available, but the most common one is linked to a savings account known as Save As You Earn (SAYE).

SAYE schemes have a monthly limit to encourage you to tread carefully, as it would be daft to put all your investment eggs in one basket. You don't want your savings to collapse if your employer goes bust or if you're made redundant.

Some employee share option schemes aren't a perk. They're a danger – especially in small companies whose prospects sound brilliant (on paper, at least). It's easy to be lured from a well-paid, secure job into risky employment with the promise of share options sometime in the future but a greatly reduced salary now. Most option plans lock in employees for a number of years; by the time they take their options, the shares could be virtually worthless, assuming that the company is still in business. Putting all your eggs in one basket is always an error, so never tie your fortunes so closely to one company. No matter how attractive the deal sounds, a wage packet bird in the hand is worth several options in the bush.

Five Basic Investment Choices

All your money decisions, outside of putting your family fortune on some nag running in the 3.30, simply involve making up your mind as to where to put your money. Literally tens of thousands of choices are available. At least a thousand choices are in most daily newspapers.

But you can cut that number down to just five possibilities by considering basic investment choices only. Get these right, or even just right more often than wrong, and you're well on the way to financial success:

- ✔ Cash
- ✔ Property
- ✔ Bonds
- ✔ Shares
- ✔ Alternatives

Here's a big investment secret: most professional fund managers – yes, those City of London types who pull in huge salaries and even bigger bonuses for playing around with your pension, insurance or other investment money – don't wake up each morning asking themselves which investments they should be buying or selling that day. Instead, they reduce the investment world to five big buckets that they call *asset allocation*, which simply means that they divide up investment money into the five areas I've listed above – cash, property, bonds, shares and alternatives. They take your money and allocate a portion to shares, another portion to property and so on. The fund managers, and the people who run large pension funds, know that if they get their asset allocation decisions right and do nothing else, they'll beat the averages over the long term.

Can this theory fail? Yes, especially over the short term, by which I mean up to two or so years. In the great financial crisis that started in 2008, almost everything went down. You couldn't just move from one thing to another because whatever you switched to was equally under pressure. No single investment theory works all the time. The best I can do is to point you to those that have a good chance of working most of the time.

You can't go wrong with cash

Having cash under the mattress, or anywhere else at home, can be very comforting when everything is going wrong in your life, but it isn't a good idea from a security point of view. Nor does it make sense for investors. Putting your cash in a bank protects it from thieves, fire risks, and perhaps the temptation to grab it and spend it in a shop.

You never earn much money just leaving your cash in the bank. Most bank account money is in current or cheque book accounts, which often pay just 0.1 per cent, an interest rate that, transformed into pounds and pence, gives you the princely sum of £1 for each £1,000 you have in the bank for a full year. And if you're a taxpayer, that £1 may be worth as little as 60p after HM Revenue and Customs take their slice. Ouch!

Better ways of investing your cash that you don't want today are available, including building society deposit accounts, online cash accounts, telephone banks and postal accounts. With all these options, you can get a higher interest rate but you have to give up flexible access to your cash in return.

The longer you're prepared to tie up your money, the better the rate of interest you'll receive. You can lock into fixed rates so you know exactly where you stand, but you must be prepared to hand over your money for a set period, usually one to three years, and throw away the money box key. Granted, some fixed-rate deals let you have your money back early, but only if you pay a big penalty.

The whole point of cash investing is to use it when you're uncertain or everything in your life looks awful. It's a security blanket you can retire to during periods when all else is confusion or contraction.

Don't disrespect this fact. Keeping a firm hold on what you have isn't just for fast-falling markets. It's a vital concept in the months ahead of retirement or any other time when you know you'll want cash and not risks. You lock in the gains made in the past and can go ahead and plan that big trip, your child's wedding or the boat you want to buy. Cash is what you can spend, and expenditure is the endgame of investment.

Property is usually a solid foundation

The property you live in is probably your biggest financial project – assuming that you don't rent it from someone. Typical three-bedroom semis now change hands at £300,000 or more in many parts of the UK. And at the higher end of the market, no one blinks an eye any more at £2 million homes.

But is property an investment? Yes, because you have to plan the money to pay for its purchase, buying can help you spend less than renting and because you can make or lose a lot of money in property.

Property beyond your home can also be a worthwhile investment. Stock market managers run big funds like property because it rarely loses value over longer periods, often gains more than inflation and provides a rental income as well. Commercial property, such as office blocks, shopping centres, business parks, hotels and factories, is usually rented out on terms ensuring not only that the rent comes in each month (unless the tenant actually goes bust) but also that the rent goes up (and never down) after each five years, when the amount is renegotiated.

Bricks and mortar are as solid an investment as you can find outside of cash, as long as the bricks and mortar are real. A fair number of property schemes take money from you for buildings that only exist on the architect's plan. This is known as *off-plan purchasing*. In many cases, these buildings eventually go up, although you might sometimes struggle to find a mortgage lender or a tenant – or both. Some don't, however, and these cases leave you nursing a loss as the developers and their agents gallop off into the sunset with your cash. This bad buy-to-let industry reputation puts off many mortgage lenders even where the building is finished to specification. Additionally, problems with loans can also make tenants wary – they know they can be evicted if landlords don't have satisfactory financial arrangements.

Besides building up value in your own home, you have three main routes to invest in property:

- ✔ **Buy to let.** You become a landlord by purchasing a property that you rent to others.

- ✔ **Buy into a property fund run by a professional fund manager.** You can do so through personal pension plans, some insurance-backed savings plans and a handful of specialist unit trusts.

  ✔ **Buy shares in property companies.** This is the riskiest method but the only one that can provide above-average gains.

Every week I get emails offering me 'guaranteed returns' from property or forests or farmland in some distant country. In many cases, the returns are promised over ten years and are truly enormous. I always delete these as trash. A 'guarantee' is only worth as much as the organisation backing it. And I don't reckon much on the chances of an offshore company being around in a few years' time, let alone paying me what it promised.

Bonds are others' borrowings

A stock-market-quoted *bond* is basically an IOU issued by governments or companies. Loads of other sorts of bonds exist, including Premium Bonds, which give you the chance to win £1 million each month at no risk. But here we're talking bonds from governments and firms, which go up and down on stock exchanges.

Bond issuers promise to pay a fixed income on stated dates and to repay the amount on the bond certificate in full on a fixed day in the future. In other words, you pay the government, say, £100, and the Treasury promises to give you £5 a year for the next five years *and* your £100 back in five years' time.

Sounds simple, right? Well, it's not at all. Bonds are complex creatures with many traps for the unwary. (I devote a big slice of this book to the ups and downs of bond investment.) But if you reckon price rises will be kept to a minimum and interest rates will stay where they are or go down, then bonds are a good bet if you need regular income.

Bonds are becoming more common as well. The reason is partly because many investors have been taken with the relative safety and steadiness of bonds compared with shares and the relatively higher income they offer compared with cash. (Everything in investing is relative to something else, by the way.) But the reason is also because the people running big pension funds need the security and regular payments so they can afford to pay cheques each month to the retired people who depend on them.

The easiest way to buy into bonds is through one of the hundred or so specialist unit trusts. But don't take the headline income rate they quote as set in stone. It can go up or down, and there are no guarantees or promises. Some even cheat by hiding costs away. Always remember that the capital you originally invest in the bond fund isn't safe either. It can go down or up along with investment trends and the skills of the manager.

Get your share of shares

Shares make up the biggest part of most investment portfolios. They can grow faster than rival investment types and produce more. They're probably your best chance of turning a little into a lot – even if the first decade of this century was a shares disaster.

Shares are what they say they are – a small part of a bigger picture. Buying shares (or *equities*) gives you partial ownership of a company. You can own as little as one share, and if that's the case and the company has issued one million shares, you have a one-millionth stake in that enterprise.

You can't chip off that one-millionth portion and walk away with it. What you get is one-millionth of the profits and a one-millionth say in the future of the company. But you won't have a one-millionth share of clearing up the mess if the firm goes bust. You can never lose more than you put in.

Ownership rights are becoming more important and more valued. Put a lot of small stakes together and companies start to notice you, especially if you have a media-attractive project, such as protesting against excessive pay for fat-cat executives who fail to deliver anything to shareholders and then collect big bucks when they're sacked.

Most shares are bought because owners hope that they'll produce more over the long term than will cash, property or bonds. They generally have done this, although no guarantees exist. Shares are your best chance for capital gains and the top choice if you want a portfolio to produce a rising income. But take heed: they can also be an easy way to lose your money.

Want to know the most dangerous sentence in investment? 'It will be different this time.' Sometimes, that becomes 'the new paradigm'. What they mean is that they have found a magic formula to find an investment that goes up but not down. That sentence is trotted out whenever prices rise rapidly and brighter investors start to question how long it can continue. The thing is, it never is different. Anything that people promise is a one-way bet is bound to run out of steam sometime, whether you're looking at property prices, the price of wheat or shares in African economies. Share prices, and the values of every other single investment in this book, go up with greed and down with fear. As long as these human emotions exist, 'It will be different this time' will be the same nonsense as the last occasion it was trotted out. Expect to hear this phrase many times during your investment life!

Alternatives are a hodgepodge to consider

This investment area covers a rag-bag of bits and pieces. For some people, alternative investments concentrate on items you can physically hold, such as works of art, fine wines, vintage cars, antiques and stamp collections. But for an increasing number of people, the term means hedge funds, which are about as esoteric as investment gets. Put simply, you hand over your money to managers who, by hook or by crook, hope to increase it.

In most cases, don't even ask how those types of managers hope to gain cash for you. They won't tell you. Or they won't be informative, instead just coming up with some meaningless jargon phrase. And don't even ask what will happen if they fail. They don't like to talk about this possibility, even though you could easily lose all the money you have with them.

So is there a plus side? Yes. Hedge funds are the only realistic way you can make money out of shares when prices are falling all over the place.

You can't invest directly in a hedge fund unless you're really rich. Some funds work on an invitation-only basis, so you wait until you're asked! But you can sometimes put your money into a fund of hedge funds. This is a special vehicle that buys, holds and sells hedge funds, and they're sometimes offered to the general public – or at least those who can afford the minimum £7,000 they usually require.

One new alternative is the wonderful world of commodities, where you can bet on the price of anything from potatoes to potassium, from sugar to silver. Commodity investment looks like soaring into fashion. Some people will make a lot; others will lose their shirt. But no one can foretell who, when and where. That's the fascination of investment.

Chapter 2

Recognising What Makes an Investor Tick

---

*N*eedlework and carpentry are among the skills where you need a firm hand and a good eye as well as technical ability. You need technical ability in investing, too. But instead of the firm hand and the good eye, you need an understanding of investor psychology – how you tick and how the other investors who make up the market tick as well. This chapter looks at psychology – but don't worry, you don't have to read huge tomes or understand long words.

Good investors know all about the mechanics of buying and selling stocks and shares. They know how to tell a positive company balance sheet from a looming disaster. And they understand that a relationship exists between interest rates, inflation and what they earn on their investment cash.

Great investors do all that *and* something more, something far more vital. It doesn't involve learning how to interpret share earnings forecasts, how to understand credit risks, or how to evaluate the future of small companies. What it involves is far more basic – and far more essential. This extra something is investor psychology, and it's what this chapter is all about. I tell you what investor psychology actually is and explain some specific emotions that make an investor tick. I also explain that although gambling and investing share certain similar characteristics, they're actually very different ventures. For those whose emotions range from cautious to scared stiff, I provide some starting-point investing advice.

Understanding Investor Psychology

Investor psychology comes in two parts – the psychology of the marketplace and the psychology of the individual. This section helps you understand each part.

The psychology of the marketplace

Both small and big investors used to direct research toward where companies were going, what their likely future earnings would be and what shape their business would be in three to five years into the future. Investors still do this research. But a new dimension is appearing in stock-market analysis, especially that coming from the United States. This new way of thinking recognises that even the brightest and best investors make mistakes and lose money when they should have made profits. Why? It could be because their judgement was clouded by the comfort of being with the crowd or by hating the idea of standing alone or by refusing to accept early enough that they made an error. In other words, they went for the comfort blanket of conformity.

You need to stand back from the crowd and its noise. Instead of following the herd, understand how it works so you know where investment values are going and why. Winners think 'outside the box'.

The psychology of the individual

Knowing how you'll react to what goes on in investment markets is vital. As you read this book, you'll experience some very basic emotions, such as 'I'm comfortable with this' or 'I wouldn't touch this investment with the proverbial bargepole' and a whole range in between.

Couple these emotions with setting your own investment goals. Depending on the sort of person you are, your goals could range from the reasoned ('I want to make my spare cash grow a little over the next five years') to the 1 in 10,000 chance ('I want to quit work in three years' time and live on a paradise island').

Working out where you are on the line that goes from a need for complete comfort and security to wild gambling enables you to make more rational decisions, including probably the most important one – the decision that at times it's best to walk away. The psychological aspect of investing is what separates figuring out investing from figuring out plumbing or gardening.

Looking at the Emotions That Drive Investors

Two specific emotions drive investors to make the decisions they do. These over-riding emotions are greed and fear. Everyone has both to some extent or another. Knowing the effects these feelings can have on investors is a powerful tool.

Greed is the accelerator

Greed is what you want that goes beyond pure need. Granted, negative connotations are sometimes associated with greed, but consider these facts: without the greed for more and better food, we'd still have the monotonous diet of cave-dweller times. Without the greed for spices and other trea-sures, Columbus would never have set out for the East and landed in what became America. And without the greed to go faster, we'd all still be on foot. Greed drives us forward. But no two investors act identically.

Fear is the brake

People often ask me why share prices move so wildly during a very brief timescale when little, if anything, has changed in the underlying company. They also want to know why downward movements tend to be more violent than upward gains. I reply that the stock market is like the first day of post-Christmas sales in posh department stores. If someone shouts, 'Designer frocks are reduced by another 75 per cent!', there's a big rush to the women's clothing floors. That's the greed factor in action. But note that not everyone joins the rush. Men, for example, just stand and stare.

But there's another factor to consider. If someone at that same posh department store shouts, 'Fire!', (or the alarms ring) then *everyone* rushes for the exits. That's the fear factor in action. And it takes only one or two people to panic for even more people to panic, thus reducing the hope of an orderly evacuation. The result? It could take some time for that store's reputation as a safe environment to return.

Coming full circle here, the scenario is much the same with investment markets. And the point I want to stress is that fear is a stronger emotion than greed. When fear, justified or not, gains the upper hand, pandemonium can break out as investors rush for the exit and the safety of other investments.

So, as an investor, how do you deal with the market pandemonium caused by fear – and with the prices that are falling all around you? Well, first, know this fact up front: when a real stocks and shares panic is going on, don't even think about beating the professionals to the selling exit. Their training makes them faster and heavier than you. And they have a direct line to the stock-broking professionals who'll deal with their £10 million selling order before they even pick up the phone or look at the screen for your £1,000 worth of business.

So if you can't beat the herd as it thunders to the exit, you need to develop other strategies for the inevitable bear markets. (Falling share prices are known, for reasons now lost in history, as *bear markets*. Investors who think prices will fall are *bearish*. The opposite, rising share prices, are called *bull markets*. Optimists are, of course, *bullish*.)

Here are some strategies to consider (check out Part II of this book for specific directions on buying and selling shares):

- ✔ Sit tight. If you don't need to sell, don't. You don't make a loss until you sell. Paper losses are just that.

- ✔ Look at your investments and assess whether they're directly affected by whatever is behind the panic or whether they're just being pushed along by the market as a whole.

✔ Be counter-intuitive. Use the panic to buy selected investments at knock-down prices.

✔ Consider potential tax bills if you decide to sell. The UK's capital gains tax can take up to 18 per cent of your profit.

✔ Use the bear market period to hone your research. Filing away all the negatives that come out during this time is valuable for future reference in a bull market, when all you hear is positive talk.

✔ Don't sit up all night worrying. It won't help!

Here are some tips to keep in mind during this tough time:

✔ Time is the healer. Share prices have always eventually recovered in major markets such as the US and UK, although you'll have to be patient.

✔ You're probably still earning dividends from your shares. These regular payouts will often hold up better than the share price.

✔ If you fancied an investment at £1, it could be better value at 75p, assuming nothing else has changed.

✔ This year's big losers are often next year's major gainers.

Debunking the 'Stock Market as a Casino' Psychology

Stock-market columns in newspapers often refer to investors as *punters* and talk about *having a fun flutter*. So it's not surprising that many people see the stock market as a giant casino, admittedly without the overblown decorations of the Monte Carlo model. And, you can take bookie-style bets on stock-market moves.

It's true that you can make some comparisons. For example, in the stock-market casino, you pay your admission fee in the form of brokerage commission (the percentage you pay a stock broker for working for you) or upfront charges on an investment fund, and your fate is decided by the roll of a dividend increase (that's good news – it means you'll get a bigger cheque for the shares you own) or a cuts-in-earnings warning (markets don't like companies that let you think they'll do well and then change their minds). You can also make some superficial comparisons, not the least of which is that when you lose, all you have to say is that the fruit machines were coming up with lemons instead of plums. Regardless of these comparisons, gambling and investing are very different ventures. This section sorts out the differences.

How things work in gambling

In gambling, you're totally dependent on some random acts. For example, in a roulette game, you have no control over the wheel and no way of knowing which number will turn up after the wheel stops spinning. All you can do is ration out your bets in such a way that you minimise your losses.

You may gain in the short term on a few lucky choices. But if you play long enough, you'll lose, thanks to the zero on the wheel, because when it turns up, the house wins everything bet on black or red, on odd or even and on individual numbers. Because zero turns up once in 37 times, it's equal to chipping away approximately 3 per cent of all the money bet. Wheels that contain a double zero, well, they double that tax.

Consider for a minute another gambling game – the fruit machine. In theory, the fruit machine is a zero-sum game. It can only pay out what's been put in. But even optimistic gamblers know that those machines are built to repay only about 80 per cent of what's put in, so the casino company is bound to win. It's said older machines are even meaner!

How things work in investing

Investing is different from gambling. You aren't totally dependent on random events like the drawing of a card or the spinning of a wheel. You know beforehand many (although not all) facts about where you're placing your money. Your skill comes from evaluating these facts and then allowing a percentage for the unknown.

Equally important, time is on your side. You aren't forced into an instant appraisal. No one is (or shouldn't be) hassling you to make a decision on what to do with your money. And the game isn't over when the fruit machine shudders to a halt, the roulette wheel stops spinning or the cards are put face up. Stocks and shares have long lives – most have no set expiry date. As an investor, you always live to fight another day unless your investment goes bust.

But most important of all, investment isn't a zero-sum game. New money comes into the market all the time. New investors put in fresh cash, and in addition, either knowingly or from pension-fund deductions, the companies into which you buy also put fresh money into the equation through dividend payments on shares and interest on bonds.

Most investors just look at the share price but ignore the dividends – the half-yearly (sometimes four times a year) payments where companies divide out part of their profits for the benefit of shareholders. That's a big mistake. Money is money wherever it comes from. All those small amounts add up to big cash over time. Always remember that a dividend bird in the hand is worth a lot more than *maybe money* in the bush.

Two dangers investors share with gamblers

Even though gambling and investing are two different ventures, two dangers exist that investors sometimes share with casino-frequenters.

The gambler's fallacy

The *gambler's fallacy* is that the past can affect the present and the future. Say, for example, that you have a £2 coin fresh from the mint. You toss it once. It lands heads up. What will the next throw bring? You have no idea. So you toss the coin again, and it lands heads up again. How will it land next time? You're not too sure, but you think it might land tails up. After all, it's landed heads up twice and the coin is perfect. But it doesn't. And with each successive head, you get more desperate and your belief grows that it should go to tails.

Suppose, also, that you're betting on these tosses. With each loss, you double up your original stake in an ever more desperate attempt to make your fortune. After ten losses in a row, your original £10 bet has become £20,480. The coin has no memory so each subsequent toss has no relationship with the previous. True, tails will come up some time, but can you afford to wait? That's the gambler's fallacy in action, and the negative result it can bring.

You can see the gambler's fallacy in investments. So-called experts quoted in newspapers say the market is going up (or down). On what do they base their assertion? Often it's no more than that the direction last month has to repeat itself this month; or that it's time the market changed direction. Distrust this – it's no different from the coin-tosser hoping for tails after a run of heads or the coin-tosser who believes that a run of heads will result in another head.

The gambler's fallacy is also present when so-called stock-market historians attempt to call the market by reference to the number of months since an event took place. History tells you about the past. And it suggests that all empires eventually crumble. But could anyone have used the timing of the Roman Empire to predict how long the British Empire would last?

Overconfidence

Overconfidence leads you not so much to magnify possible gains but to minimise the effect of losses. 'It can't happen to me' is how people express this kind of overconfidence. But, oh yes, it can. Overconfidence can also cause you to keep increasing your investment stakes to recoup previous losses. Doing so is easy if you trade electronically via the Internet. Just a few clicks and you've committed yourself to a deal.

Combine the gambler's fallacy with overconfidence, and you could move into short-term investment tactics such as spread bets and options and be asked to pay out more than you've invested.

Trading too much can backfire!

One of the wonders of investing is that the fundamentals driving those involved – a mix of greed and fear – never, ever change. So although the following case comes from a 1998 study by researchers Brad Barber and Terrance Odean and is based on American experience, the story is as relevant today and in the UK as it ever was.

The researchers showed how many investors earn poor returns because they overtrade with too many buy-and-sell decisions. They make matters worse because they tend to go for smaller companies that are both more volatile – that's bigger ups and downs – and cost more to buy and sell.

Barber and Odean looked at the trading records of 60,000 small investors in the US. They found that these individuals managed to beat the averages of all share prices and indexes such as the UK's FTSE 100 (the *Footsie*) or the US Standard & Poor's 500 by 0.6 per cent per year. Not a lot, no, but it builds up to big sums over a lifetime of investing. So far, so good.

Now for the bad news. Because these investors tended to buy and sell often, and because the gap between the price at which you buy a share and that at which the share is sold to you is wider in small-company stocks than big-company stocks, the average investor paid more than 2.4 per cent of his money into trading costs. So the original 0.6 per cent gain turned into a 1.8 per cent loss per year. What's worse, the most enthusiastic traders lost 5.6 per cent in costs, so they underperformed the averages by 5 per cent per year.

For some investors, overtrading occurred because buying and selling shares had become a hobby, and those investors had become addicted. Psychologists say that over-activity is a way some people control their environment. But sadly, this psychological requirement some people have (and it's close to compulsive gambling) runs counter to the need for good money discipline.

The moral? Don't overdo share buying, or trading in and out of collective investments such as unit trusts or investment trusts. Each time you switch, there's a cost. In the UK, the cost is stamp duty and maybe capital gains tax as well. So always think before you swap investments. Doing it occasionally is fine because you've come up with good reasons for your decision. But buying and selling can eat into profits.

Chapter 3

Squaring Risks
with Returns

*W*hen we walk down the street or drive a car, we're aware of risks. We know, for example, that we might risk life and limb crossing a road when the red man symbol is displayed. And we know that our safety (not to mention driver's licence) is threatened if we drive 60mph in a 30mph zone.

Granted, if we run helter-skelter down the street or drive recklessly down the road, ignoring everyone and every rule, we might arrive more quickly at our destination. But the faster we go and the more corners we cut, the greater the chance of losing everything. So we generally take simple precautions to avoid risks. That way, we make some progress through life.

But what if we never took risks at all and, instead, wrapped ourselves in cotton wool? If we only walked on perfectly kept, deserted fields and drove on empty roads at exactly 10 mph? We'd simply not get anywhere, and our lives would be boringly empty. We'd be taking the risk of missing out on something interesting and perhaps profitable.

The same can be said about investing. Investment risk is no different from the risks of daily life. There are steady-as-you-go investments that give a moderate rate of return with perhaps the occasional loss (after all, even the most careful driver can have a bad experience). There are hell-for-leather investments that can offer massive returns or huge losses. And there's the investment equivalent of surrounding yourself with layers of cotton wool – where nothing will happen at all.

In this chapter, I examine investment risks – specifically, the benefits and drawbacks of various investment possibilities and ways to increase your odds of successful returns.

Examining Two Investing Principles You Should Never Forget

Here are a couple of clichés that sound banal but should be carved in mirror writing on every investor's forehead, so they can read them each morning when facing the wash basin:

- ✔ *There's no gain without pain.* In your daily life you have to move out of the couch potato position to achieve.

- ✔ *You have to speculate to accumulate.* If you don't take chances with your money, you'll never get anywhere.

Financial markets – indeed, all of capitalism – work on these two principles.

Here's an example to help you see the importance of these two philosophies. Suppose that you're running a company and need £10 million to finance a new product. You could borrow the money from the bank, knowing that you'll pay 10 per cent interest a year whether the new venture works or not. If this new venture fails, you still have to pay the bank its £10 million plus interest even if it means selling the rest of the business. But if your business idea turns out to be a winner, the bank still only gets its £10 million plus interest while your fortune soars.

Alternatively, you could raise the cash through an issue of new shares, where the advantages for you are no fixed-interest costs and, if the project is a flop, your investors suffer rather than you. They could lose all their money. That's the risk they run. But if the venture is a success, the shareholders receive dividends from you and see the value of their stake rise due to everyone demanding a share of the action. You shared the risk with others, so now they get a slice of the reward.

Now suppose that no one had taken any risks. You decided not to expand into the new product. The bank manager vetoed all loans. And the share buyers sat on their hands and kept their money. There'd be no pain – no one would lose – but there'd also be no gain for you, the bank, the investors or the wider economy. Either the new idea would never see the light of day or someone else would do it instead. Granted, all these potential participants could've argued that they'd taken a risk-free stance with their cash. But had they? No. They'd taken the severe risk of missing out on something positive. They didn't speculate. They didn't accumulate.

Determining the Return You Want from Your Money

The starting point of any risk–reward assessment is to determine the return you want from your money. The harder you want your money to work, the more risks you need to take.

You may want your money just to maintain its buying power – to keep up with inflation. Or you may want to see it grow in real terms by a relatively small amount – just enough to keep ahead. Or you may want some aggressive growth to fund a pet project. Suppose, for example, that you have a 10-year-old child who's been given a £10,000 lump sum by an adoring relation who had one proviso: the money must be spent on university education when the child reaches 18.

The most basic education costs £10,000, but most will need more – especially if they wish to study for a post-graduate qualification. So what rate of return over the eight years would you need to produce the result you want? Inflation, which erodes your target figure in real spending terms, investment fees and taxation have been ignored here to simplify the figures:

£10,000: 0%

£12,000: 2.31%

£14,000: 4.3%

£16,000: 6.05%

£18,000: 7.62%

£20,000: 9.05%

£25,000: 12.14%

£30,000: 14.72%

£35,000: 16.95%

£40,000: 18.92%

The higher figures – those over that needed to produce £18,000 – are more than what you're likely to earn on your money unless

✓ You're prepared to take big risks, including losing your original capital

or

✓ Inflation returns with a vengeance so you appear to obtain substantial gains even if they don't translate into real spending power at the shops.

Investments are for the medium to long term – from five years upwards. So, over this timeframe, what can you expect? The following sections tell you.

The likely return from shares

Anyone reading newspaper headlines or watching television news can be forgiven for believing that shares only go in one direction. And that direction goes through 180 degrees from time to time. It veers from 'everyone pile into a one-way bet' to 'run as fast as you can from shares'. Oddly enough, the euphoria tends to come after a big price rise while the misery memoirs all too often come after a huge fall in values.

This tells you two things. Firstly, the media fail to present a balanced view. Secondly, and more importantly, the media fail to understand that shares work for the long term.

Shares are volatile, but over the very long term, say the whole of the last century, a basket of typical equities has produced average annual gains of around 12 per cent before tax.

Using different start and finish dates can produce almost any other figure you care to think of. But however you cut it, the trend in share prices is upward provided that you're patient. No one would bother to take the inherent risks with shares if they didn't expect to make greater gains than with bonds, property or cash over the longer term.

The return from shares comes in two forms, although neither is guaranteed, let alone even promised:

✔ Dividends

✔ Capital gains

Dividends are the way companies have of returning part of the profits they make, or the reserves they've built up over good years, to the part-owners of the firm. That's you, the share-holder. These are small amounts compared with your initial investment. But if reinvested into more shares, they can boost your holding. A 3 per cent annual dividend, after any tax, rein-vested would add around 40 per cent to your shareholding after ten years.

The beauty of dividends is that you should get them whether share prices as a whole are going up or down. Dividends are regular, and a company cutting out or missing a payment is a very bad sign indeed. Oddly enough, missing dividend pay-ments was the only thing Northern Rock didn't do as it fell from grace in 2007. Even when Northern Rock was in severe trouble, the bank maintained its ambition to pay shareholders their twice-yearly cheque. The payment was only cancelled when it was pointed out that this dividend would have been paid from rescue money supplied by the Bank of England. This was fur-ther bad, but unsurprising, news for shareholders.

The second return from shares is that the capital goes up. Is this a sure thing? No. But should it happen? Yes, although only over the long term. The last decade has been a shares disaster and the only one since the Second World War where shares fell after inflation.

What you get from a share depends on the exact price you paid and when you purchased. If you bought at the top of the market and the share then halves in value, it could take the best part of a decade before you're back on the growth track.

The likely return from bonds

Are you an avid reader of Victorian novels? If so, you know that the heroines always know the value of the hero's (or villain's) fortune by turning his lump sum wealth into so much per year. And the figure selected is always 5 per cent because this was the long-term return the Victorians expected.

And how do heroines of Victorian novels always know this? Because in Victorian days, most money went into bonds. Those from the government were the safest. Those from railway companies and iron works were riskier. So although the Victorian novel heroine may not be able to recognise all that much of the world around her, she is at home with the finances on bonds.

Nothing much has changed. As a result, her 5 per cent isn't a bad long-term guess for today. You'll get a little less if you head for the super-safety of UK government bonds, or *gilts* as they're known in the money trade. And you'll get a percentage point or two more if you aim for *corporate bonds*, bonds issued by commercial companies raising loans.

But how do you get the 8, 9 or 10 per cent on offer from some bonds and bond funds? Easy! You just aim at bonds – known as *junk bonds* – from firms that have a dodgy track record. In addition, the bonds of some countries have junk status because the country's underlying finances are a mess. Nations from Latin America or south-east Asia have often been guilty parties.

If you're willing to take the risk that they'll miss a payment or, worse, fail to give back your capital on time or at all, you may be rewarded for your bravery by the potential doubling of your return over safe bonds. But although you may end up with more, you may equally get your financial head blown off in a crisis. And there have been plenty of those.

Investors who like to sleep at night should look at bonds paying out a maximum of 5.5 to 6 per cent. Bond fund purchasers should go no higher than 4.5 to 5 per cent. Why the gap? Because the fund carries an annual fee, typically 1 per cent, which must be paid out from somewhere! These costs come directly from the bond's income, hence the reduction.

The likely return from property

According to the Nationwide Building Society, the average price of a modern property throughout the UK was around £163,000 in early 2010. In 1992, the price of that same typical home stood at £51,630. Track back to 1983, and it was just under £26,000. And three decades or so ago in 1973, it was £9,800. Sound like the prices only go upwards? Not true, because in October 2007 the average stood at £186,000.

But for the purposes of this discussion, leave aside what you might make from your own home, because you have to live somewhere, don't always have much choice on where you live and would be paying rent if you weren't buying. Instead, think in terms of commercial property.

Professionals invest in commercial property, such as factories, office blocks and shopping centres. You can't go out and buy a business park unless you have tens of millions and the ability to manage your investment. But you can tap into commercial property through a number of funds.

What you get from a property investment comes from two sources. One source is the rent tenants pay. You won't get this straight into your pocket, though. You'll have to fund management costs, repairs, interest on borrowings and tax. The second source is the hoped-for gain in the underlying value of the buildings. Add the two together, and you get the full return.

Since 1971 the overall annual returns from property have only declined in six separate years according to figures from experts Investment Property Databank. These were the financial crisis in 1974, three years during the economic downturn at the start of the 1990s, and in the years 2007 and 2008 when almost everything went down.

In present-day conditions, you can expect to earn around 6 to 8 per cent a year averaged over long periods. So you can expect more from property than from bonds but less than from shares. However, you don't need to repair a bond, have security guards for bonds or worry about a bond going out of fashion. And properties come with more expenses.

Commercial property is different from domestic property. Figures for the two seldom go in tandem.

The likely return from a cash account

Don't expect too much from a cash account. Many pay a pittance – and that's before tax. You should only invest in cash for safety, never for the long term unless it is of paramount importance that you know exactly what you will have in the future to meet a known financial need such as a child's education.

Since 1971, cash has only been the best performing asset type during two years – 1974 and 1990. And both years, the financial system was in trouble. Cash was the worst place to put your money during at least 12 separate years. Over almost any long period, cash has been easily out-gunned by bonds and property, and it's been beaten out of sight by shares.

The likely return from other assets

Investors have seen spectacular returns from gold, diamonds, works of art and even special shares offering guaranteed tickets at the centre court at Wimbledon for the All-England championships. Others have made big money out of race-horses, vintage wine and stamp collections. But all these ventures demand a whole lot of specialist knowledge combined with a whole load of luck. Fans of this sort of thing tend to flag up the good times and ignore the bad years.

Figures are fairly unreliable because you're always comparing apples with bananas. A painting by Pablo Picasso may double in value over a year, but that doesn't say anything about a Salvador Dali or even other works by Picasso.

Many illegal investment schemes have been offered in areas such as stamp collecting and fine wines. These schemes offer big gains for supposed small risk. The authorities have shut down some of these ventures but usually not before hapless investors have lost their savings.

Increasing Your Chances of Successful Returns

Risk and reward, risk and regret can't be separated. You must take risks and put your head above the cash investment parapet if you want to win.

Now turn risk on its head and call it opportunity. It's really the same thing, but now you have a positive phrase. You can increase your chances of success by diversifying (not putting all your investment eggs into one basket) and being patient.

Plenty of factors affect your chances of success

Suppose that you acquire shares in ABC Bank and XYZ Insurance, perhaps as a result of free share handouts. Obviously, you have to work out whether the opportunities in each company are worthwhile. And that's something I look at in detail in Part II.

But for now, you need to consider the bigger picture altogether. No company is an island, and none lives in a vacuum. Plenty more factors can enhance your opportunities or increase your chances of making a mistake:

- ✔ **Currencies.** Foreign exchange markets can have an impact on your investment. They have a habit of moving in slow trend lines, although they jump about at the umpteenth decimal place all the time. Each day, even each minute, exchange rates can go either way by very small amounts. There are no investment straight lines!

- ✔ **Interest rates.** You may invest in a brilliant company, but if interest rates go up, it will be less attractive because the cash it needs from the bank for expansion will cost it more. Rising interest rates are bad news for almost everyone other than holders of cash.

- ✔ **Stock markets.** When share prices are generally booming, even badly run companies do reasonably well. And when share prices are falling, the best organised firms with the greatest prospects tend to lose out.

✔ **Inflation.** Nope. Not car tyre pressure but rising prices. Inflation can be good for some sectors, such as retailers, because it takes the pressure off, meaning they don't have to run perpetual sales and price cuts.

✔ **The economy.** You can't really beat it. If it looks good, everything shines; when it turns down, only a handful of assets manage to hold their heads up.

Diversification is your best friend

Diversification is putting your eggs in many baskets. So if you trip up and choose a poor investment, you still have some capital left to help your finances recover. Or at least, that was what people thought before the credit/banking crisis in 2008. Now everything is up for questioning – including some of the assumptions I've made. Fact is, no one knows when or whether what previously passed for normality will return.

Both investment professionals and academics are trying to find a new way forward. And they have still to discover it. So, in the meantime, it could still be better to diversify than to stick everything in one asset type.

Understanding the multi-layered approach that professionals use

Professional investors consider what the fund they manage is supposed to achieve. If the fund's main role is to provide a regular pension income for those whose retirement needs it has to meet, the fund goes in the main for safer assets, such as bonds, property and cash. But if the fund advertises itself as a route into, say, higher-risk Far Eastern share markets, it must be largely restricted to these investments, with a little cash to give it flexibility.

Those running a fund with a wide remit, such as a life-insurance-with-profits fund (the basis of many retirement and endowment plans as well as the cornerstone of investment bonds sold to older people), work out their asset allocation as percentages of the whole fund between the main asset classes, including shares, bonds, cash and property.

Within each of those asset areas, they then buy a wide range of investment assets. The idea is not to be caught out if one area catches a cold. Within property, for example, a fund manager may buy some office blocks, shopping centres and industrial premises. Within shares, a well-diversified fund manager may have holdings in the UK, the US, mainland Europe and the Far East.

Wide-remit managers then further subdivide. Say, for example, that a fund manager has holdings in the UK, the US, mainland Europe and the Far East. Regarding the fund focusing on UK shares, the fund manager may decide to have a percentage in different stock-market-company sectors, such as bank stocks and engineering companies.

Only after looking at all those various things do fund managers look at individual shares, deciding to hold pharmaceutical company A rather than B.

Concentrating too much on one or two investments is a mistake. Another mistake is not looking at all your wealth. If your pension fund is riding on UK shares, then you should consider other points in your own investment strategy for money under your direct control.

Spreading your money in practice

Suppose you had £1,000 in 1971. In addition, assume that you managed to avoid the temptation to spend it all and invested it instead. And, to simplify matters, say that you had a choice of just four investments – cash at the building society, UK government bonds, a commercial property portfolio and the UK stock market. The results have been widely different. The time-frame is well over the span of a generation, so plenty of ups and downs have occurred. They are all well documented by Barclays Bank offshoot Barclays Capital in its excellent annual number-crunching exercise, whose figures I mostly use here.

If you'd put all your money into a cash fund, your £1,000 would've been worth £24,000 by the end of 2009. That sounds good, but that figure is before the taxman has taken his substantial slice. Putting your money into government bonds would've netted you a more respectable £43,800. Property would've fared even better – around £46,000, or even more in hotspots such as central London. And despite the up and down nature of shares, an equity portfolio would've been valued at £106,000, again not counting tax.

Now, had you been really cautious and divided your money into four equal parts for our four asset classes, you'd still have a considerable £54,950, or more than five times the amount you would've needed to keep up with inflation. Most of the gains would've come from shares despite their poor performance over most of the past ten years.

But what if you'd been a real speculator, believing that you knew the best of the four each 1 January for the following 12 months? If you'd perfect foresight, your £1,000 would've grown to over £2 million. Yippee!

And, finally, what if you'd got it wrong each time, picking the following year's disaster zone? You would have around £500 – just around a half of what you started with. What would've bought a new car in 1971 is now just about enough for a medium-priced pushbike!

One thing all the figures show is the power of re-investment. If you'd spent your money as you earned it rather than putting it back, your fortune would be a tiny fraction of these figures – whatever investment you chose.

Patience is your pal

To be a good investor, you need to have a good strategy and good diversification, but to be a savvy investor, you also need patience and time. Your investments may need years to mature. There may be more days when your investments go nowhere or down than when they rise. But when they do increase, it can be by substantial amounts over a short time.

Your own time horizons determine the risks you can afford to take. Investment is not a short-term punt on financial markets. It requires at least five years, preferably longer. Short-termism can also increase your costs and your tax bill.

Chapter 4

Being Aware of Small Print – and of Print that Isn't There

In This Chapter

▶ Knowing that shares can go down as well as up

▶ Knowing that bonds can go bust

▶ Understanding that super-strategies can turn into sand

▶ Being aware that property investments can crumble

▶ Avoiding the tax-freedom trap

▶ Putting a stop to scamsters

So you've taken a long, hard look at how ready you are to take the risks inherent in investing. You know that you have to take chances and step, a little or a lot, into the financial unknown. And you know that if you aren't prepared to take a risk, you stand no chance of beating the bank or the building society. And now you've made up your mind to invest rather than merely save. (If you *haven't* taken a long, hard look at these things, then you really, really need to. Look through Chapter 1 to make sure that you're even ready to invest and check out Chapter 3, which is all about investment risk.)

Congratulations on making an informed decision. Now you have just one hurdle to cross before you're ready to look at the nitty-gritty of investing. That one hurdle is getting into the habit of reading the small print in investment situations before looking at the headlines. You're in the right place because this chapter tells you all about those nasties.

'Um, Where Do I Actually Find the Small Print?'

Small print exists in virtually all investment situations. You'll find the small print in places like the bottoms of adverts and way down through official documentation. Small print is virtually invisible for a purpose. It has to comply with the law (which has never defined how small is small) but does not draw attention to itself.

At times, you won't always understand what you read. When that happens, ask the person you're buying from. If the reply is still incomprehensible, then shred the deal. Plenty of other opportunities are out there with words that make sense.

Know that if small print exists, you'll be deemed to have read and understood it, even if it's located on page 199 of a document and written in language only the lawyer who wrote it could possibly follow. The Financial Ombudsman Service (the last port of call before court for complaints about financial products) won't look kindly on you if you complain that you lost your money through not reading the small print, although you might have some cause for complaint if the full version of the legal stuff was not made available or if it really is gobbledygook.

Shares Can Go Down As Well As Up

Seems simple enough: shares can go up and down. Yet that information has taken many people by surprise because they'd been lulled into a false sense of security by the silver-tongued investment sellers who convince customers (and possibly even themselves) that share prices will go on rising forever. 'Treat any price reverse as a reason to buy more,' they say. Remember that it's the investment seller's job to sell investments just as it's the farmer's job to produce food.

You need to be prepared for the value of your shares to go down, and the small print in investment documents addresses this very issue. The wording is often something like this: *The*

*value of your investment and the income you receive from it can
go up or down, and there is no guarantee you will get your full
investment back.*

Of course, shares can go up too! Individual shares can go to
zero, but shares as a whole have never become worthless in
any one country outside of cataclysmic events such as the
Russian Revolution back in 1917.

Even the best companies' share values go backwards when
shares are falling all around. Sometimes the top companies
suffer unduly. When share purchasers want out quickly, they
sell the good stuff first because the rubbish is harder to shift.
(Think of which properties in your area would be easiest and
quickest to sell if the owners needed to raise cash.)

Besides being prepared for the value of your shares to
go down, be aware of the following truisms about past
performance:

- ✔ **Past performance isn't necessarily a guide to future
  performance.** The Financial Services Authority (FSA)
  says that there's no relationship between the future and
  the past. All too many funds like to sell their wares on
  the basis of past performance, and they show this in the
  most flattering light (surprise, surprise!). Investment
  companies not surprisingly disagree with the FSA
  because they spend a fortune advertising their past successes, hoping customers accept that the future will be
  the same. Academic research supports the FSA line, with
  some experts reckoning that the past of a fund has no
  more relevance to the future than using past winning lot-
  tery numbers as a guide to winning the next draw.

  Three degrees of falsehood exist: lies, damned lies and
  investment statistics from companies trying to sell you
  something.

- ✔ **Past performance may not necessarily be repeated.**
  Even if an investment remains successful, it's not likely
  to be successful in the same way as before. The investment may do better or worse. In any case, it all depends
  on which time period you use for the comparison.

In recent times companies have started to tell investors more
than they used to reveal. They update more often and are
under a duty to comment on unusual share price moves (even

if it's to claim they have no idea what's going on) and to 'correct' market assumptions such as forecasts of future earnings made by stockbrokers' analysts. These usually take the form of a *profits warning*, serving to dampen down expectations. Companies would rather ease investors down gently over a few months rather than let them fall with a big bump. Equally, although this happens less often, firms that are doing better than the market predicts will tell investors to upgrade their forecasts.

The Best Bonds Can Go Bust

Fixed-interest securities, or *bonds*, can fail to pay their regular promised income or the final repayment of the original capital, a scenario called *default*. You need to be aware that the higher the payout, the greater the chance of a default. Here are some bond warnings that you'll find in bond-fund literature, and sometimes in the legal material that accompanies a bond issue. You won't find anything about these risks if you simply buy a bond through a stockbroker.

- ✔ *This fund invests in higher yielding bonds (non-investment grade).* The risk of default is higher with non-investment grade bonds (also known as junk because they could go bust or fail to pay out on time) than with investment grade bonds (they're the ones from really respectable governments and top companies). But what you can't know is how much higher this risk will be. Seasoned investors can remember Argentina defaulting on its bonds, and many Russian bonds went bad as well.

- ✔ *Higher yielding bonds may have increased capital erosion than lower yielding bonds.* This small print means that your chances of losing serious money are greater with higher yielding bonds.

- ✔ *The level of income on offer could indicate a likely loss of some of your capital.* Some bonds offer a high income now but with the chance (or perhaps almost certainty) of capital loss later on. This may not matter to some pension funds, but it could be bad news for your tax bill because you have to pay income tax on the income you get but can't claim anything back if you make a loss when you sell the bond or it comes to the end of its life.

Great Ideas Don't Last Forever

The investment world is full of bright ideas that once worked but no longer do. You won't receive any specific warning about this fact, so you need to be aware of it all on your own. Not to worry. That's what I'm here for. A couple of examples will help you understand what this concept is all about.

One now-defunct investment firm came up with a bright idea. It had a list of 30 big company shares, and it looked at which shares offered the highest dividend payments for a £1,000 stake. The firm decided to hold for one year whichever three shares fitted this recipe on 1 January each year. Then, 12 months later, the firm would repeat the whole exercise. At that time, the firm would sell shares that had moved out of the target area and buy whatever new high-dividend payers suited its formula.

When this idea was launched, it could be shown to work using historical data, a process known as *back-testing*.

The firm then stretched its initial idea so investors would get five shares that most fitted the profile and then shrunk the concept to just one share a year.

Moving the goalposts like this usually suggests desperation on the part of the concept's promoters. They move the goalposts so you hopefully don't notice that their scheme isn't making money. Surprise, surprise. High ones, threes, fives (as these schemes were called), and probably any other number they might've come up with all failed to produce the desired effect.

What worked in the past has no more chance of working in the future than any other idea.

Another brainwave was the January effect. Someone noticed that shares went up in January, so an idea was born: buy the day or so after Christmas Day. Problem was, once the idea got around, it ceased to work. Clever share buyers decided to anticipate the January effect by purchasing equities *before* Christmas. Then another group decided to pre-empt those clever share buyers by putting in orders at the end of November. Give this practice a few more years and it would've got back all the way through the year to January!

Once an idea is known to more than a tiny handful, it ceases to work.

Property Investments Can Crumble

Whether you read it or ignore it, a lot of small print exists around bonds and shares. But when it comes to property, hey, you're out there on your own. There's scant documentation for you to consider, even for those with the sharpest eyesight.

So here are the warnings property purveyors would put in, if they were obliged to do so:

- ✔ *No one might want to live here.* The danger here is when a new project doesn't attract any tenants or doesn't attract tenants of the quality and deep pockets expected.

- ✔ *No one might want this property in the future.* Properties fall out of fashion. I can't be the only person to live near a 1930s shopping area that once hosted top retail names but now is a mix of low-rent takeaways, even lower-rent charity shops and zero-rent boarded-up premises.

A good property fund or property company whose shares you've bought will work all this out and so come up with a value for the building or rent for the tenant that better reflects reality. Low rent is better than no rent; £5,000 per year rent on a property without bank debts that cost £5,000 to build decades ago is a lot better than £10,000 rent on a new building in hock to the banks that cost £100,000 to build. However, property funds have a small-print clause that allows them to freeze investors into the fund when the going gets really tough, meaning that anyone 'wanting out' has to wait until the managers allow them to escape.

Plenty of property opportunities aren't well managed or require you to put all your bricks on to one site without diversifying your risk.

Property sales people get their money from selling you real estate. Once they have their commission, they're unconcerned about what happens next.

Tax-Free Can Be a Dead Loss

I hate paying taxes. You hate paying taxes. Anyone who can legally cut their tax bill generally tries to do so.

The government has a number of legitimate tax-saving schemes, primarily pensions but also Individual Savings Accounts (ISAs), which are intended to encourage people on modest incomes to put money away for the future. Also available are a number of more obscure schemes involving everything from high-tech start-up companies to conifer plantations. The rationale for some of these schemes has been lost in the mists of antiquity.

'Tax-free investment' or 'pay no tax with this plan' are such powerful draws that they're featured as huge headlines in a large number of investment ads. The idea is to grab your attention. But there's hidden subtext you need to know about.

Some investment-product firms use tax benefits as a 'feel the width, never mind the quality' approach. These sellers hope that you'll be so impressed by the chance to get one over on the taxman that you won't look too closely at what they're really pushing. So be very aware of the following:

- Product providers and sellers use phrases such as 'government-approved tax savings' to imply that the scheme has state approval or that it's as solid as the Bank of England. But in reality, the tax benefits are a few pennies a week and the risk is still there. If your investment falls, you won't get any government handout.

- The advertised tax benefits may only apply to a minority. Sometimes, they may be positively harmful to others. For example, non-taxpayers can actually lose out on some deals because they can't claim anything back. HM Revenue & Customs (a.k.a. HMRC or the taxman) reckons that if you pay no tax, you can't get a refund.

- Many tax deals come with a deadline. Product providers know that no one wants to miss out on a bargain. They hope you'll buy in a last-minute rush and, again, not look too critically at what's on offer.

The worth of any ISAs held on your death count toward the value of your estate and any inheritance-tax bill. So if HMRC doesn't grab your money while you're living, it will collect from your estate when you die. Great thought, that.

Foreign Scam Operations Are Bigger (and Trickier) Than Ever

All previous sections of this chapter paint a grey picture, meaning they warn you that promises of top investments can actually prove to be average or just plain mediocre investments. But this section paints a flat-out black picture, meaning it warns you of scamster investments that guarantee you'll lose every single penny. You may even lose more if you're persuaded to run up a big credit card bill in an attempt to get your money back. You won't. You'll just be even poorer. But despite the fact that many are run by organised crime, the mob just loves the veneer of respectability, so some of these scams come complete with their own warnings. So just like the more legitimate investment plans, they can say you should've read the small print.

With a particular type of scamster, you're dealing with organised crime that makes the bad guys in *The Godfather* films look like amateurs. This crime was perfected in Toronto in the 1970s. Now, it's bigger and nastier than ever.

The scam can start with a simple letter. It may say that you're an investor in a company, which it names, and that you might like to receive a special research report on that firm, compiled by investment experts. Or the letter may be more general, simply offering a regular investment newsletter compiled by experts. The report or newsletter is, of course, free.

Those who reply are required to give details, including phone numbers. The company's return address is often in the UK, although that means nothing because it's just a mailbox. A UK phone number is equally meaningless because diverting calls to somewhere way beyond UK legal protection is easy. In addition, the company isn't regulated under UK investor-protection laws so you can't go complaining to anyone.

An alternative is an email approach, where you're offered a free report on a currency or stock market, always supposedly compiled by expert analysts. A third approach the scamsters use is to send millions of junk emails (they're usually sent from Asia or Eastern Europe) lauding the prospects of a company you've never heard of. The scamsters try to cover themselves by revealing that the email senders were paid a sum such as $30,000 for their work.

However they do it, the scamsters now have your interest. Often, they leave you alone for some weeks to receive your newsletter. You may notice that 75 per cent of the four-page letter is devoted to mainstream shares and economics. But the back page gives lavish praise to the money-making opportunities in a share you've never heard off, usually with a high-tech or scientific bent. They use all this stuff for the next stage of suckering cash from their victims.

Here's the really dangerous bit unless you're prepared: the scamsters (invariably men) phone you. The firms, known as *boiler rooms*, may state that they're based somewhere like Beijing, Barcelona, Belgrade, Mexico City or Mali. It doesn't matter. Wherever they claim to be and wherever they really are (rarely the same place), it's outside UK jurisdiction.

Now for the sting. The caller may make some pretence at discussing your investment needs, but he's really trying to probe how much you can be taken for. The representative tells you that you could be in a great investment that could double your money in 30 to 60 days, or make ten times as much by this time next year. It's a straight appeal to greed, and it works because these firms continue to proliferate. Of course, the shares are worthless and you never see your money again.

Scamster representatives use hard-sell tactics to persuade you to buy the shares, commodities, currencies, precious stones or works of art they're touting. The FSA is aware of *experienced* investors who've been pressured into buying things from these representatives, which shows how persuasive these salespeople can be. If the representative sells you a commodity or currency deal, he may call you back soon after with news of your winnings. The purpose is to persuade you that the firm is safe and that you can make easy money. Don't bother asking for your winnings back in cash, however. You'll never get them. They'll suggest you re-invest. If you insist on your money, they'll ignore you, and because you won't be able to find them, they'll pocket your money. But if their appeal to your greed works and you want more, the scamsters will just 'trade' your cash until they have it all.

Alternatively, the representative sells shares in a tiny company, usually one with a miracle cure or technological wonder. Invariably, the boiler room buys the shares at their true worth – usually one-tenth of a US cent – and sells them to you at $1 each (boiler rooms always use US dollars). They're *restricted shares* too, meaning that you can't sell them without the company's permission (never forthcoming) until a year has passed, by which time the company will have disappeared, assuming, of course, that a real company was there in the first place.

After buying the shares, you generally experience delays and difficulties obtaining your share certificates. The shares turn out not to be the great deal you were promised. When you try to sell the shares you're usually told to wait a few weeks because important news, which will transform the price, is about to emerge. This is another tactic to keep you holding on.

But even if you do appear to have sold the shares, you nearly always have difficulty obtaining the proceeds or are put under pressure to buy other shares from the same boiler room with the money, so you never get to see the cash. Or you may be contacted by an organisation with another name that offers to get the money back provided that you pay an upfront fee.

These follow-up firms are known as *recovery rooms*. They're usually linked with the boiler room that ripped you off – otherwise how would they have all your details? But linked closely or not, their aim is a second bite at your bank account. The usual story with the recovery room is that it has an investor prepared to pay $20 a share to acquire the whole company. Now, as you've only paid $5 a share, you're convinced that this is the miracle exit you've been waiting for. You calculate that you'll have made $50,000 profit. There's just one piece of paperwork to complete, the recovery room tells you, and a share transfer fee of $10,000. Pay that and then the 'buyer' and the recovery room both evaporate with more of your money.

No one contacts you out of the blue for your own good. Stick to what you know.

Part II
Shares and Bonds

'I ignored the rumours about the recession sweeping the city, and now <u>I</u> am.'

In this part . . .

Are you interested in how financial markets operate and in figuring out ways to analyse markets and companies? If so, this part is for you. I explain what you need to know about how stock markets work.

I cover in detail what shares and bonds are, how to invest in them, and some of the advantages of ownership. I take you on a tour of world markets and examine the UK stock market up close. I tell you where the stock market entry routes are and provide tips you can use when you're ready to invest. I explain that being a successful share investor involves looking at numbers from stock-market-quoted companies and help you understand what those numbers mean. And I explain how important information-gathering is and tell you how to build your own information bank.

Chapter 5

Comprehending How Stock Markets Work

* *

In This Chapter

▶ Unravelling the mysteries of shares and your ownership rights

▶ Explaining bonds and the rights you don't get

▶ Looking at the basics behind price rises and falls

▶ Discovering whether you can predict price moves

▶ Going behind the scenes to see how the stock market operates

* *

*A*ll financial strategies, including those to keep all your money in cash or property, are based on what happens on stock markets – they're the big drivers of the world's finances. But stock markets can appear to be places of great mystery – even more so nowadays because most don't really have a physical presence at all.

This chapter unravels the mysteries of the stock market. I explain what shares and bonds are. I spell out the reasons for the ups and downs of the market and offer tips for predicting market moves. And I describe the basic mechanics of the stock market so you can better understand those newspaper columns or online blogs you read every day.

Looking at the Evolution of the Stock Market

For centuries markets existed where items were bought and sold. Many of them, such as cattle and other livestock markets, were open to public scrutiny. They didn't require membership or passing exams. All people had to do was walk in with some money, and they'd walk out with an animal – or vice versa. If they knew what they were doing, the deal worked. If not, they ended up with the famous pig in a poke – not a good idea.

Markets in companies started off in the same way, often in City of London coffee houses. But they became specialised as more sophisticated companies were set up that needed to raise money from investors. Share dealing had to be centralised (helped by inventions such as the railway and telegraph).

Once centralisation happened, share-dealing became the plaything of the professionals who did what all professionals do – setting systems to ensure that they kept the work for themselves at the terms they considered suitable. Stockbrokers formed partnerships and controlled the work through the stock exchange, which they collectively owned.

Life carried on like this until the mid-1980s, when the City found itself in the midst of a huge change in working methods. Out went the cosy arrangements of the past and sleepy stockbrokers who worked from 10 to 4 with three hours for lunch. In came big banks, big money, long hours and a sandwich lunch at your desk, if you were lucky.

In addition, out went the old stock exchange, where the public could watch goings on from a viewing gallery. Now, no actual place as the stock exchange or stock market exists. Everything's traded electronically. All you get to see in a stockbroker's office is an ocean of trading screens covered in a tidal wave of numbers.

But the fundamentals of what makes markets tick haven't changed. And another thing hasn't changed: rising shares are shown on screens in blue; falling ones are in red. These colours are just as they were in the old days when prices were displayed using coloured chalks.

Understanding Shares

A *share* is literally that – a share, or part, of a company. And if you own shares, you have a stake in the fortunes of the firm involved and a say in its control, in proportion to the number of shares you hold.

BT, for example, has over 1 million UK shareholders. All bar 7,000 hold fewer than 10,000 shares. But although nearly all the shareholders are small, it's the big investors who really control things – in the case of BT, the major investors own about 85 per cent of the company.

Never get misty-eyed about your shareholder rights in any big company, such as voting or attending annual meetings. They rarely add up to a row of beans.

Shareholder democracy and shareholder power only works for major investors, who are sometimes called *activists* because they buy big slices of a company so they can influence the directors to do what they want. This isn't always in the best interests of other, less well-organised shareholders.

How companies get to the stock market

The process of bringing a company to the stock market is more complicated and vastly more costly than bringing a cow to a cattle market. The process involves lawyers, accountants, investment bankers and public relations specialists. They all take big fees, often adding up to tens of millions of pounds in a big company, because they need to feed their expensive salary habits.

The process of bringing a company to the stock market used to be known as a *flotation* but now it's more likely an *initial public offering* (IPO). Effectively, they're one and the same. The IPO is accompanied by a ferocious amount of documentation known as a *prospectus*. It gives you the following:

- Details about the company, its past performance and prospects for the future (including profit forecasts).
- A full balance sheet.
- The past records of directors and senior managers (including any disasters they've been involved with).
- Pay packages for the top people and details of any deals between directors and the company.

> ✔ The advisers, such as brokers, banks, accountants and lawyers, used by the firm. The quality of these advisers is important. If some or all of them are small or not generally known, or have a past poor reputation, the IPO could be criticised.

Large companies often bring their business to the stock market through a public offering, so anyone can apply. This is how most of the privatisation shares were sold.

Smaller firms often use a device called a *placing*, where they offer large parcels of shares to selected stockbrokers and investment banks who then distribute them to clients. This method has the disadvantage of locking out other investors but the plus point of a lower cost. If you invest through a collective fund such as a unit or investment trust, you might end up with some of these shares in your portfolio.

Note that some companies list on foreign markets (that includes overseas firms listing in London and UK firms going for overseas market quotes) when they want to extend their shareholder base, because some investors are limited to buying securities traded in their own countries or don't want the inconvenience of dealing with overseas-based equities. This doesn't usually involve existing shareholders, although it's claimed that a wider base makes the shares more attractive.

Ways to buy shares

Buying shares through an IPO is usually a good deal. One reason is that they're cheaper, because you have no brokerage fees or stamp duty to pay. In addition, companies like to bring their shares to market at a little less than the amount their advisers consider fair value. They want the headlines to say 'first day big share price advance' because an early gain grabs investor attention. They don't want stories that warn 'overpriced shares going down'.

An IPO should also signal a particularly good time for the company. It would fail completely if the prospectus were riddled with profits warnings.

Regardless, an IPO is no guarantee of long-term success. And watch also for directors and other large shareholders using a flotation to unload millions of shares for cash. If they had faith in the company, they'd want to hold on to as many shares as possible.

Sometimes, huge numbers can benefit from an IPO. Back in the late 1980s, the Abbey National was a building society owned by its members. But at that time, it decided to become a stock-market-quoted company. It gave each of its qualifying members a set number of shares in return for giving up their membership rights. These people received 100 shares worth £1.30 each. The company also sold additional shares at the same price to these investors. These shares are now part of Banco Santander, the Spanish bank that subsequently bought Abbey. Some of those former Abbey savers still have shares in Santander.

Companies can issue more shares later on, offering them to all shareholders through a *rights issue*, which gives every shareholder the right (but not the obligation) to buy shares in a fixed ratio to their present holding, usually at a lower price, or discount, to the then stock-market value. So if a company launches a one for four issue, someone with 400 shares can buy up to 100.

If you're attracted then you have to send a cheque for the full value. But if you can't afford them or don't want any more of that company's shares, you have two choices:

- ✔ You can sell your allocation as *nil paid rights*. This works on the basis that although you haven't paid for the shares, you own them until the closing date for the rights offer so you can sell them in the stock market to someone else who's willing to pay for them. You end up with a cheque but pay no dealing charges.

- ✔ Sit back and wait for a cheque. If you do nothing, then your allocation will be added to all of those that aren't taken up and sold in the stock market after the rights issue period finishes. You'll get per share whatever big investors were prepared to pay. Obviously, the more successful the company and the more attractive the terms of the rights issue, the more you'll get.

Firms can also issue shares to pay for companies they acquire, so those firms' former owners acquire equity in the new company instead of a cash payment.

The shares most people buy and sell, though, are properly called *ordinary shares*. Some companies have an additional type, known as a *preference share*. Note that ordinary shares are often called *equities*, but they have nothing to do with the UK actors' union Equity! In the United States, shares are usually referred to as *stock* or *common stock*, but the principle behind them is the same.

Companies may offer other investment possibilities, such as bonds or loan stocks, but ordinary shares, or equities, are the most frequently traded. They're also potentially the most profitable and, also, the most at risk.

Equity holders only receive a dividend after other classes of investors, such as bondholders, have been paid. And they're last in line for a payment if the company goes bust. They usually get nothing in that event. But equity holders are the legal owners of the company. They get all the earnings of a successful firm after obligatory payments to loan stock and bondholders. Equity holders take the lion's share of the risks, but they get the lion's share of the rewards.

Understanding Bonds

Lots of financial bits and pieces are called bonds. Many come from life-insurance companies. Some come from the sometimes febrile minds of the ever-inventive people who work in marketing departments. Others are Premium Bonds, a once a month National Savings & Investment flutter. The word *bond* even sounds reliable. The reason is because of all that old stock-market stuff about 'my word being my bond'. But in this book I don't focus on those bits and pieces called bonds. Instead, I cover *bonds* that are loans made to a company or government that can be traded on stock markets.

Governments have raised money from citizens and others through loans called *bonds* for centuries. Now companies increasingly get cash by issuing bonds instead of, or as well as, shares.

A bond promises a regular and fixed interest payment and repayment of the original amount on a set future date. Between the date the bond is acquired and that of its final repayment, the bond's price goes up and down according to circumstances.

Owners of company-issued bonds, usually known as *corporate bonds*, must be paid before equity holders if the company is in a sticky financial situation. If the firm goes bust, bondholders will probably lose their money, however.

Chapter 9 deals exclusively with bonds, when you're ready for detailed information on the subject. For the purposes of this discussion, I just want to point out the perks you *don't* get when buying bonds:

- ✔ Bondholders don't get the right to attend annual general or extraordinary general meetings (although most companies don't object) unless the meetings are labelled as specific meetings for bondholders.

- ✔ Bondholders can't legally put questions to directors, although nothing stops them from acquiring one share to do so.

- ✔ Bondholders don't receive an annual report as a matter of right.

- ✔ Bondholders can't apply for more shares if the company launches a rights issue.

- ✔ Bondholders generally have no rights when another company tries to acquire the firm via a takeover bid.

- ✔ Bondholders don't receive larger payments when the company does well.

Getting Familiar with the Ups and Downs of the Market

Every day, many newspapers carry hundreds, and often thousands, of share and bond prices. The Internet offers access to tens of thousands more, often changing prices not just once a day, like print publications, but as changes happen (often with a 15-minute delay).

Prices go up and down most days, if not most hours. Shares of the biggest companies with the greatest number of shareholders are the ones whose prices move most frequently. These shares are called *liquid* because prices flow easily with buying and selling orders.

Smaller-company shares are less liquid or often illiquid. Dealing is less frequent, but when it happens, the effect is far more pronounced.

Why do prices move? It's the most frequent question investors pose, and it's the most difficult to answer. And even when the answer is obvious, such as a price rise due to the company announcing a juicy new contract or a price fall due to the company losing a juicy old contract, it's not so obvious why the price has changed by the percentage it has.

Not to worry. This section helps you sort out the reasons for market ups and downs.

Why do prices rise and fall?

A market truism is that prices rise because there are more buyers than sellers. Don't take that literally, though, because sometimes there are a few large buyers and thousands of small sellers. But if the number of shares buyers are bidding for exceeds the number holders who want out are offering for sale, the price rises.

This stuff is basic supply and demand. If the demand from buyers is high, the price rises to persuade more holders to sell. This situation continues until buyers believe that the price has risen far enough or, as happens often in markets, too high.

Keep in mind, though, that supply and demand trends in stock markets are far from those neat supply and demand graphs you see in economics textbooks. Prices often tend to overshoot in one way or another but they do that all over the place – look at oil prices, for instance, where in one recent one-year period they went from $145 a barrel to under $45 and then rose again.

The law of supply and demand, or the balance of buyers and sellers, is always there. What investors must do is calculate the plus and minus factors for any equity or bond.

Looking at specific and systemic risks

A share price is an amalgamation of many factors – some applying to the company you buy into and others applying to the stock market in relation to the general economy at the time. Factors that apply to the company itself are called *specific risks*. Factors that apply to the stock market itself (and thus to all shares) are known as *systemic risks* or *market risks*.

Don't forget that risk can be good or bad. All the word means is that prices may go up or down more than you might otherwise expect or be comfortable with. Risk isn't a word of abuse like *dodgy* or *dishonest*.

In fact, professional fund managers can even invest in *volatility* – that's the amount a share or share price index moves either side of a fixed point. If you're interested in how this works, check out the VIX index. High VIX readings mean investors see significant risk that the market will move sharply, whether downwards or upwards. A low figure indicates steady as you go. Some investors confuse risk with fear, but the VIX can be high because share buyers expect prices to zoom. Risk or volatility is really just another unknown to add into the share price equation.

A share in Real Ale Breweries PLC, for example, (not a real company, but one that I've made up) carries specific positive risks, such as a hot summer pushing up sales, beer becoming more fashionable, more pubs and shops stocking the brewery's products or someone discovering that a pint of beer a day (or more!) is good for your health. The brewery also carries specific negative risks, such as the directors running off with the takings, health warnings on beer, new taxes on alcohol and drinkers switching to wine.

Systemic risks are different from specific risks. When prices are generally rising, and every evening TV news bulletins end with an increase in the FTSE 100 (the Footsie) share index, almost all shares go up by some amount – even those with just mediocre prospects. And when prices fall, a large number of shares go down, although not all. You can sometimes spot a strong company because it holds up when prices are falling all around.

You can never totally isolate the systemic risks from the specific. But if you buy individual shares, or subscribe to a fund that does so for you, the underlying quality or rubbish status of an equity usually works through eventually. A top-class company may fall in a collapsing market but less steeply than others. And when the recovery finally comes, it will gain more quickly and more strongly.

Much share analysis is concerned with relative values rather than absolute gains or losses. A share or fund that falls 10 per cent when the index or average of all funds loses 30 per cent is considered a success, even though you still lost money. Likewise, a share or fund that goes up 10 per cent when the index or average gains 30 per cent is considered a flop despite your profits!

Looking at factors that can make share prices rise

Here's a checklist of factors that can cause a share price to rise. Use this list every time you think about buying into an equity to see how many factors apply.

Nothing ever happens in isolation, so never fixate on one point alone when considering whether to buy an equity!

☐ Investors in the company believe that a takeover bid is likely for the company whose shares they own.

☐ The company has a major new contract.

☐ The company has a big new product.

☐ Prices for what the company does are going up fast.

☐ The company has a new dynamic director.

☐ The company is expected to make record profits – more than previously forecasted.

☐ The company looks more lowly rated on its likely future than rival companies.

☐ The company earns a lot of money from importing, and foreign currencies have fallen in value against the pound.

☐ The company earns a lot of money from overseas operations, and the pound has fallen against the principal currencies in which it does business.

☐ The company has a lot of bank borrowings, and interest rates have fallen.

☐ The stock market overall looks like rising, and this share usually goes up faster than average shares in the market as a whole.

☐ The company is about to win a major legal battle.

☐ The company intends to raise its dividend by more than average.

☐ The company has plans to cost-cut by shutting down unprofitable parts of the business and sacking superfluous staff.

Looking at factors that can make share prices fall

Many of the factors that cause prices to fall are the reverse of those that make prices rise. Other factors apply only to falling markets. And the last one in the following checklist has a special perversity of its own:

☐ Bad publicity is expected. For example, the company is responsible for an environmental disaster, or the accountants have been caught falsifying figures.

☐ The stock market is in a bad mood, and this share usually falls faster and further than the average.

☐ Figures show that trading is bad in the company's main business area.

☐ New government legislation will add to costs or force the company to operate in a different way.

☐ The company has launched a takeover bid for a rival company, which could turn into a battle involving an auction set to get out of control.

☐ The company, to raise money, is issuing millions of new shares at less than the present price. This will 'dilute' your holdings.

☐ The company's product range has been criticised as being out of date or technologically inept.

☐ The company's credit rating falls with international bond assessment agencies.

☐ The company issues a profits warning.

☐ A takeover rumour turns out to be wrong or a takeover approach collapses.

☐ The company is seen as sound but unfashionable, so the hot money moves to hot (and often over-heated) sectors.

☐ The company says that the dividend will be cut or not paid at all.

☐ There's an absence of news and/or investors perceive the company as being boring or forget all about it and thus divert their investment money to rival firms.

Can anyone predict these moves?

Billions of pounds a year are spent on stock-market analysis. Extremely highly paid people examine every nook and cranny of bigger companies, consider the economic wider picture and look at any other factors they consider relevant. And that's *before* fund managers enter the scene. (*Fund managers* are professionals who buy and sell shares on behalf of clients and big financial institutions. They focus their efforts on pension funds and unit trusts so they have their take on what they think is going on.)

Some market analysts get it right more often than they get it wrong, but many have less than a 50 per cent success record. This outcome sounds like they don't earn their money, and to be truthful, some don't deserve what they get. The difficulty all analysts face is that what moves markets is a sense of surprise – happenings either good or bad that haven't yet been factored into the equation. All they can do is to point out what is known. They know unknowns exist!

Stock-market operators are remarkably good at reacting to news. The share price often changes in seconds. But after an 'event', the market adjusts either up or down, so it's too late. After news is revealed, these facts are referred to as 'in the market' or 'in the price' (both phrases mean much the same), and the share value has changed to take account of it.

Take a look at the checklists of factors that can cause prices to rise and fall (located in the previous section). At any one time, some or all of those factors are the subject of comment or a news release. It's only when these factors change for the better or the worse that prices will move – going nowhere or coming in exactly as predicted will leave a share price static. Of course, this is about specific risk – systemic or market risk is far more down to big economic factors. So when banks were going bust in late 2008, prices fell across the board.

One way to predict market moves is to have enough information sources so you can spot a trend before others do, and especially before the company has to reveal it.

What smart investors do

To predict market moves, smart investors can look for new products, scour the trade press and Internet sites to find details of potential new contracts or, on the negative side, try to spot early signs of consumer discontent.

One way to spot changes before they're officially announced is to get inside information from someone working for the company, a practice known as *insider trading*. It's illegal as soon as an investor tries to profit from it. The illegality applies whether the investor works for the company or simply knows a source of factual material.

The authorities have rarely been successful in prosecuting insider trading. The reason, in part, is due to the way insider traders hide their tracks through offshore companies in exotic locations where there's little, if any, regulation. But the reason is also due to the difficulty of proving something in a market where so much rumour and tittle-tattle exist, ranging from the totally accurate to the downright and intentionally misleading.

'But 1 don't have time to do all the stuff professionals do!'

You have a number of disadvantages compared with professional investors, including an almost certain lack of time and resources. Unless you give up your day job (definitely not advised!) or are retired (then only invest money in shares you can afford to go without!), you won't be able to spend hours on end looking at share movements and company announcements. And if you can afford the battery of screens the professionals use, then you're too advanced and too wealthy to need this book.

You also won't have access to all those big ticket brokers trying to sell you services by offering research into markets and individual shares. Nor will you be able to call on in-house analysts and economists.

But don't worry. No evidence exists that all that material actually helps professional investors with the right calls. Instead, all that material acts as a prop and an excuse when things go wrong, as they inevitably will.

As a private investor, you *do* have a number of advantages. These days, with the availability of the Internet, any investor can know what's happening with a given share or market almost as soon as the professionals with their batteries of screens. Online services offer information for free with a 15-minute delay or instantaneously for a fee. And with online dealing, you can respond almost as quickly.

You can't definitively predict market moves. But neither can the professionals. You have the advantage, though, of being able to set your own investment agenda. This could include your ability to simply ride out price falls. After all, you don't have to worry about three-monthly reviews or the chances of being sacked as a fund manager.

Understanding the Mechanics of the Stock Market

Most small investors stand well back from the day-to-day, hour-to-hour and minute-to-minute goings on in the stock market. They do just as well, if not better, following this course. But short-term movements can sometimes add up to a long-term trend, and understanding basic UK stock-market mechanics will help you make sense of those newspaper and online columns that discuss daily ups and downs.

Most markets are made up of four levels: the producers and the product, the middleman, the retailer, and the consumer. In the vegetable market, for example, the producer is the farmer; the middleman is the wholesaler at one of the big central markets, such as New Covent Garden in London; the retailers are greengrocers or supermarkets; and the consumer is you.

Stocks and shares are no different. The product is the tiny part of the company represented by each share, the middleman is the market maker, the retailer is the stockbroker and the ultimate consumer is you.

How big money moves big money

Around 80 per cent of the value of the London stock market is owned by big investors such as pension funds, insurance companies, unit trusts and investment trusts. They don't really own it, of course, because they're merely working for the real owners – you and me and millions of others who've entrusted savings to them.

Nevertheless, these big investors act as though it's their money, and they're the people whose influence moves share prices most readily. They have more effect on big companies because they trade shares in these major corporations more often. Many smaller companies may have their share register dominated by the firm's directors and private investors.

You can find a daily list of trading volume in large company shares online or in the *Financial Times*. This list gives figures for the amount of shares changing hands on any day. The figure, in thousands, must be divided by two because each share will have been traded twice – once as a buy and once as a sell. Every fully quoted share can be traded every day, but volume can vary from zero (rarely) to hundreds of millions.

High volume (jargon for 'lots of trading') in a share often occurs just after a statement from the company. But if you can't see an obvious reason why shares in a company are heavily traded, make some more enquiries, especially if the price changes substantially. Look through newspaper market reports and scour Internet sites. They won't always give you the reason, but high volume should always alert investors in those shares. It could be good news if prices are higher on high volume but bad news if the opposite!

The pivot in markets is the middleman, and the stock-market middleman is the *market maker*, a market professional who assesses second-by-second the weight of buy and sell pressures and adjusts prices accordingly. This activity determines what the brokers charge you or give you when you sell – adjusted, of course, for their fees.

Market makers always try to find a price level where both buyers and sellers are satisfied at any one moment. This practice is called *balancing the book*. If more buyers than sellers exist, market makers are *short of stock*. They don't have the shares to satisfy demand. So they increase their prices to bring out sellers so they can achieve balance.

Equally, when more sellers than buyers exist, market makers are *long of stock*. Prices are marked down to entice new buyers. Market makers are no different from vegetable wholesalers who mark up prices when demand is high and mark down prices when buyers are scarce.

Buyers pay more than sellers receive. The gap between the bid (or the buying or asking) price and the offer (or selling) price is called *the spread.* The bigger the company and the more often its shares are traded, the narrower this spread is. A major company such as Vodafone or Lloyds Banking Group may only have 1p or 2p or so between the bid and offer prices. But smaller companies can have larger amounts. Note that the prices shown in newspapers and on websites are mid-prices – halfway between the bid and offer.

Chapter 6

Taking the Catwalk Route to Investment Success

- -

In This Chapter

▶ Looking at fashions and styles in investing

▶ Getting to know the UK stock market

▶ Weighing up big and small companies

▶ Taking a secret peep at how fund managers make decisions

- -

*O*ne stock-market theory advises investors to watch the hemlines of women's skirts. When they go up, then folk are optimistic and share prices will rise. But when they go down, it's a sign that harder times are coming and that share values will fall.

It sounds a load of nonsense. However, it makes some sense to link fashion to finance. Short skirts often mean free and easy living, which comes from optimism – the roaring '20s and the late 1960s are good examples. Long skirts mean the opposite – they indicate life getting more difficult. And of course, they're useful in cold climates.

Well, that's the theory, for what it's worth. But the fact is that investment styles go in and out of fashion just like the clothes you wear. And it takes a brave person to flout fashion altogether.

Equally, what goes around, comes around. When it comes to investment theories, nothing new under the sun exists because ideas go stale and then get reinvented.

This chapter looks at investment styles. And just like short skirts versus long skirts, it suggests a number of opposites. But the important thing – just like clothes – is to end up with something you feel comfortable with.

Exploring Common Investor Styles

You may think of yourself as an investor, out to maximise your money, but the investment industry likes to pigeon-hole people a little more. It divides the world into 'growth' and 'value' stock-picking styles, which I explore here. A third style also exists – the momentum investor with a shorter-term time-frame. No one style is better than another, so pick one that you feel comfortable with. And then stick to it.

Looking at performance: Growth investors

Both growth and value investors (see the following section) want their share portfolios to grow by above-average percentages. The difference is in how they get to their goal.

Growth investors look for the past to continue into the future. They search for companies that have impressed investors with previous growth – or at least the promise of it. Now, these shares don't come cheap. They're already highly rated by other investors due to their solid history of regular earnings improvements.

This means the price/earnings ratio or p/e – a key indicator to how investors see a company with the higher the number, the higher the expectation – is already soaring into the high teens or even the early 20s. And that's certainly above average. The p/e ratio is the earnings per share divided into the share price. It can be either historic (based on the last set of figures) or prospective (based on what investors expect in the future). A high p/e is said to be forward looking.

So why are growth investors prepared to buy at above market average ratings? Simple. It's because they expect these companies to continue to grow at an above-average rate. They believe the growth story is sustainable over the next one to five years. And that, they hope, will pull in other investors whose purchases will drive the share price even higher.

What do growth investors look for? High growth in the past combined with analysts forecasting growth, for starters. They want surprises – good ones, of course. They need to know that the demand for the firm's products and services will continue to outstrip the economy. And they look to see if the managers and directors are confident enough to put more of their own money into the shares. Of course, if the investors get it wrong, the downside here is that the share price could well tumble by more than they might expect.

Growth investing is a fashion. Some would never 'wear' anything else!

Spotting what others have missed: Value investors

Value investors take the view that companies exist out there that investors have overlooked. That's usually because the companies have previously disappointed investors by failing to live up to expectations. Others have simply been ignored – maybe they're too small for most professional investors or they're in a sector that's totally out of fashion.

Now, smoking is very bad for you, but tobacco shares have been great for investors. Cigarette companies were totally out of fashion some years ago. They had a product that was being squeezed by regulations including advertising bans, and it was one for which there'd likely never be a technological breakthrough. Cigarette companies weren't exciting.

The result was that the shares languished on low p/e ratios. A few investors realised, however, that all those negatives were positives. All the rules meant no new company would ever want to enter the market in developed countries. But in less-developed countries, which had a free and easy attitude to cigarettes, a huge untapped market existed of young people who see Western cigarettes as aspirational. And the lack of product progress? Great news because it prevented costly research programmes that could end in expensive disasters.

These investors took the contrarian approach. Value investors believe the rest of the market has missed a trick or three. The low p/e ratios eventually go higher.

Like growth investors, value investors reckon the share price will outstrip the current p/e rating.

Living for the moment: Momentum investors

Momentum investors are the big followers of fashion. They look for the trends, ride them as long as they're the latest big thing and hope to jump onto the next big idea as soon as the current fashion starts to fray a bit at the edges. They buy the fastest-moving shares (in the fastest-moving sector) in the belief that they'll continue to soar. The trick is knowing when to jump to the next fashion. Momentum investing is really for the screen watcher. These investors are looking for big changes over a short period – a sudden emergence from being a wallflower to being the hottest item on the dance floor. They track trading ranges and short-term growth forecasts.

Of course, momentum is great when prices are rising. But when gravity takes over, prices can plummet. However, now so many ways to make money out of falling shares exist – such as spread bets – that the thought of share price declines does nothing to deter the momentum investor.

Opting for slow and steady: Income investors

Income investors look for shares paying high dividends that they hope will be secure, although they realise this isn't guaranteed. The idea is that although they don't expect the capital value of their shares to grow at a great rate (they'd be more than happy with the average), they foresee that the dividends will add that much each year and, over time, their investment will grow to a big gain, especially if they reinvest the dividends into more shares.

Yikes! Investing styles in opposition

Although I think that the easier investing approach for most people is to take the top-down view, both the top-down and bottom-up styles of investing have their own benefits and drawbacks. Take a look at the following key points in favour of each investing style (when the opposite occurs, you get the disadvantages):

✔ Top down triumphs in times of stability and economic prosperity. When everything is progressing smoothly, investors are more willing to treat all shares and all equity markets in a similar way.

✔ Bottom up triumphs when life is uncertain. Picking winners in troubled times means you have to look at individual circumstances.

✔ Top down triumphs because it is less effort. You're only looking at markets and not the thousands of stocks that make them up.

✔ Bottom up triumphs because there'll always be winners and losers. The smart investor hopes there are more of the former!

✔ Top down triumphs because you can concentrate on the big picture and go for the 'best in class'. You think getting into oil stocks is a good idea? Then just put all your money on the best-rated oil firm.

✔ Bottom up triumphs because going for the micro view means you can look through nooks and crannies and come up with tiny firms that will grow.

This is a long-term concept. Even if the shares go nowhere fast, five years of 5 per cent dividend returns gives a good gain – around 28 per cent with compound interest. But these shares can disappoint. When times are hard, companies can slash dividends and a cut payout will nearly always equal a falling share price. So these investors suffer twice over.

Getting Up Close and Personal with the UK Stock Market

Buyers of UK shares have approximately 3,000 companies to choose from. The value of the biggest 20 of these by market capitalisation is worth more than the rest put together.

Understanding market cap

There's a huge debate in the fashion press about zero-size models (they're the skinny ones) versus plus-size (they're the more endowed women). But that's nothing as big as the continuing style debate among investors that pitches big companies against little companies – with some rooting for the middle way.

Investors measure the size of a company by its market capitalisation – they usually talk of *market cap*. It's an easy figure to calculate. You just multiply the share price by the number of shares in issue or, if you don't want to do the maths, you can find it on any one of those Internet pages that show the company's share price.

What's large, mid-sized, small or even micro cap depends on market conditions. You can't put numbers on it. But generally, the shares that are in the FTSE 100 Index – that's the Footsie that's quoted all the time in news broadcasts and newspapers – are considered large cap. That's because the rule for Footsie inclusion is based on market cap. Large companies are usually considered to be more stable (although that didn't stop some of the banks from crashing to almost nothing in 2008–2009).

The next 250 shares by size are in the midcap index – the FTSE250. And the rest, well, some are the tiddlers in the small-cap world and some are the virtually invisibles of the micro-cap universe.

Obviously, if you work for or run or own shares in one of these companies, then the micro cap is important for you. But in the big picture, you really don't matter. It's not that big investors think you're rubbish. It's the sheer cost of researching and then their inability to pick up more than a few thousand pounds worth of shares that counts against their investing.

The FTSE 100 (the Footsie)

The UK stock market's main health measure is the FTSE 100 index, usually known as the *Footsie*. The Footsie is recalculated every second, so any up or down movement in prices from trading in any of its constituent stocks automatically changes the index for good or bad. Most no-cost Internet services quote the figure (as well as share prices of individual companies) with a 15-minute delay. Services that you pay for, including some services offered by stockbrokers as part of an overall package, offer the numbers in real time.

The Footsie contains the 100 biggest UK-quoted companies by market value. The list is revised once per quarter. Companies whose capitalisations have shrunk are replaced by those who've grown larger. There's a relegation zone and a list of companies who may be promoted from among the biggest just outside the Footsie. Arrangements are also in place for immediate substitute companies if an index member drops out either because of a takeover or, less often, from going bust.

Being in the top 100 brings prestige. It also ensures a lot of buying interest from fund managers. Some funds only buy Footsie stocks; others have to keep a substantial proportion of their investment money in the top company shares both because the rules of their fund say they have to and it wouldn't make much sense for a mainstream fund to ignore all the most important companies.

By the way, savvy investors never say Footsie 100 stocks, as Footsie itself is the accepted abbreviation of Financial Times Stock Exchange 100 Share Index.

The reverse, a fall in prestige, happens if a company drops out of the list. It's often sliding down the table anyway, and expulsion adds to the company's woes. Nothing stops a company from bouncing back to the list in the next set of ups and downs, of course. A few companies have behaved like yo-yos in this respect!

Investors who look regularly at market values can often work out the likely promotions and relegations ahead of the official announcement from the Footsie folks. You just look at the capitalisations and take it from there. The advantage? You're ahead of the game, beating those fund managers, such as those running index-tracker funds who buy all the shares in an index in their correct proportions so their fund looks like a replica of the index, going up and down in line with the publicly available calculations. (Index-tracker fund rules say that managers can only buy shares after a company is firmly in the index and must sell shares only after they've been properly thrown out.)

The FTSE 250 (The Mid Caps)

Mid Caps is stock-market jargon for companies with a medium-sized market capitalisation. They're too small for the Footsie but too significant to be considered Tiddlers (see the following section for what Tiddlers are). Their measure is the FTSE 250, or the Mid Cap. As its name suggests, it's an index covering the next 250 shares after the Footsie. It contains many of the activities that are missing or under-represented in the Footsie, such as house building, entertainments and engineering. A handful of specialist unit and investment trusts focus on this medium-sized company area.

Beyond the FTSE 250: The Tiddlers

The Tiddlers are the small companies beyond the largest 100 and the next 250 that appear in the Footsie and the Mid Cap lists. Approximately 2,000 of these small-quoted companies exist, and their combined market value is smaller than the biggest Footsie company on its own. Some are former large companies down on their luck; others are companies that came to the stock market on a wave of enthusiasm that quickly ran out of steam; and a third group consists of firms with a hoped-for glittering future – well, a future one day.

Tiddler shares are unlikely to be traded on a regular basis. Sometimes it takes days or even weeks for a buyer or seller to come forward, so just one purchase or disposal order can send prices shooting upward or spinning downward. But a number of specialist funds concentrate on small-company shares, arguing that small companies can outperform the big companies because the people running these concerns are nimble enough to come up with ideas that will turn out to be tomorrow's winners.

Small can be beautiful

For many years, small companies as a group outperformed their bigger brothers. But although that outperformance was real enough on paper, investors had to be very lucky to capture it for themselves.

There were just a few front runners among the few thousand small companies. Their share prices doubled, tripled or even sextupled in a year. But if investors' portfolios missed out on them, the investors received nothing very special. Investors made a fortune out of small companies only if they were lucky or very well informed.

Since the late 1990s, the small company outperformance effect has been even harder to detect. Big funds and major stockbrokers have been unwilling to research small companies. They argue that seriously researching one small company can take as much, if not more, person power than looking at BP, Britain's biggest company at the time of this writing. It is not worth devoting loads of expensive research effort to a company worth £10 million at best compared with one valued at billions, they argue.

If you invest in small companies, you'll find few mentions in newspapers or from online sources. But they're the life blood of tipsheets, newspaper share-advice columns and a number of specialist services.

Smaller than tiddliest Tiddler: AIM

AIM, or the Alternative Investment Market, is a market regulated by the London Stock Exchange but with easier entry requirements and less demanding rules than the LSE demands. It's a bit like a golf club that lets in players with lower abilities – provided that they don't use the greens at weekends.

AIM-quoted companies vary in stock-market value from more than £200 million to under £500,000. At the top end, they could easily graduate to the main market if they wanted to. Doing so would enable them to increase their attraction to big investment managers who often can't buy AIM stocks because their fund's rules put up a bar to their investing in shares that aren't quoted on the London Stock Exchange itself.

At the bottom of the AIM list are companies worth less than a modest house in London. Most of these companies have shares whose values have plunged to 1p or even less. What these companies do is often unclear.

AIM shares vary immensely in quality. In general, they haven't performed well, although they did have a big spurt during the high-tech boom in 1999–2000. To be brutal, AIM no longer has the style cachet it once had.

Some AIM stocks have been associated with stockbrokers who've been fined and forced out of business by City watchdog the Financial Services Authority.

Here are various AIM-related titbits to be aware of:

✔ AIM shares may be quoted every day in newspapers, but according to HM Revenue & Customs and its strange regulations, AIM shares are unquoted. The reason? So that they're given a special tax status. From April 2008, this status no longer matters for capital gains tax bills, but still counts as an advantage for some inheritance tax calculations.

✔ One advantage of AIM for people building up their own companies is that they don't have to sell many shares to outsiders to achieve an AIM listing. That way, they can keep control. Whether that's good for investors is another matter. A danger is that directors will continue to see the company as their own personal toy rather than run it in the best interests of all shareholders.

✔ AIM companies are unlikely to be researched, although some brokers send out material on companies in which they or their existing clients hold a major slice of the stock. This is hardly unbiased research!

✔ The gap between the quoted buying and selling prices from market makers can be huge in percentage terms, especially for very low-priced shares. (A market maker is a professional who assesses second by second the weight of buy and sell pressures and adjusts prices accordingly. This activity determines what the brokers charge you or give you when you sell – adjusted, of course, for their commission fees.) A company with a newspaper price of 2.5p per share may cost you 3p to buy, but you'll only get 2p if you sell. So your purchase may have to soar before you can sell for the price you paid in the first place. You're running fast to stand still.

Assessing How Fund Managers Mark Their Styles

I've taken a secret peep at some internal fund manager documents. They're stamped 'not to be distributed to the public'. But I think they give such a good idea of how so many of the professionals go about their business that I have to share them with you.

They start out with three big top-down categories – shares, bonds and themes.

- ✔ Shares are subdivided by geography – United States, Europe, Japan, Emerging Markets, UK.
- ✔ Bonds are classified by risk – government bonds, investment-grade bonds from companies, high yield (that means dodgy) and debt from emerging markets.
- ✔ Themes include areas such as property, gold, commodities, medical matters and technology. Themes can be important – all of those I've just mentioned have had their moment in the spotlight (and in the investment trash can!) over the last decade or so.

Now, they split each of these categories into tactical and strategic. *Tactical* is what they expect over the next three to six months and *strategic* looks farther out. The idea is to see which have a potential upwards trend, sideways go-nowhere move or are likely to lose ground. If both tactical and strategic are pointing in the same upwards direction, that's a firm vote in favour. And if both are trending down, then it's 'don't touch them with a bargepole'.

Perhaps even worse – and this is a trap many investors fall into – is to mistake the short-term tactical trend for the long term. That way, you could easily get suckered into a tactical upswing that leads to a strategic disaster, or miss out on a tactical downturn that becomes a strategic success.

Doing all this clarifies the asset allocation decision – how much of your fortune or fund to put into the various investment classes that you started out defining.

Now, the fund managers put some flesh on these bare bones. They explain why they've made these decisions and how they'll implement them in their buying and selling.

- ✔ Tactical decisions include short-term factors such as *volatility* (how the market is bouncing around) and economic data due to be published over the next weeks. A lot of this is market noise that can hide the big picture.

- ✔ Strategic moves are based on looking ahead a year or two. Will the economy prosper or go into recession? What will the long-term outlook for currencies be? And can they learn anything from the history of the markets?

Deciphering the Greek alphabet

Fund managers and serious investors sometimes start talking in Greek. But don't worry. Their knowledge rarely goes past the first two letters of the Greek alphabet – alpha and beta.

- ✔ **Alpha:** A high alpha is good. It's a way of showing that the fund manager or the big investor has managed to outperform what would have been the result had the money gone into a passive or index-tracking fund. It's the difference between the real rate of return and the expected rate.

  Alpha is important because otherwise fund managers can collect fees for really doing very little – often for results that are worse than doing nothing.

- ✔ **Beta:** This is a measure of how risky a share or other asset might be compared with the average for similar assets. A share in the UK's FTSE 100 index, for example, would be compared for risk and volatility against the index itself. Some individual shares gyrate more wildly than the index and some less so. Investors might compare the beta of a collective fund against the average of all similar funds, or an index or whatever else is meaningful for their purpose.

  A beta value higher than one indicates a higher-risk investment that should be compensated by higher rewards. A low beta – a figure under one – means lower risk. A beta score of zero is cash in a safe bank account.

  Fund managers who come up with a low beta but a high alpha really earn their fees.

Chapter 7

Investing in Markets

- -

- -

Do you ever look through those newspaper columns headed Recent Wills? I admit I do. And I bet I'm not alone. One of the interests is seeing how much money the newly deceased but dearly beloved left behind and whether it all went to the local home for stray moggies. But the real fascination, for me at least, is trying to imagine how people who feature in the wills sections made their money. A substantial number of people made theirs from shares, often doing little more than just buying mainstream equities when they could afford them and leaving them to grow. It was a policy of benign neglect.

Trading ten times a day (or ten times a month) is bad for your financial health. The typical share purchased by an individual must go up in price around 6 to 8 per cent before you can sell it for the money you first paid for it.

These days, very few people put their entire portfolios into individual shares. Despite all the campaigns by governments and stockbrokers to increase private share ownership, a recent survey from the Office of National Statistics revealed that private investors now only own 10 per cent of the stock market, and that's the lowest ever. The figure stood at over 20 per cent at the start of 1990 when the privatisation mania was at its height. So what's happened? Well, an awful lot of privatisation shares were taken over and out of the stock market. In most cases this was because rivals, often from overseas, bought the companies. For whatever reason, most investors never reinvested the cash they got for their shares into the stock market.

This chapter provides some helpful tips and titbits as you begin investing in the stock market – so you can someday impress people – although I hope you can do this a long time before the curious read about it in Recent Wills. In this chapter, I show you routes into the market, explain the benefits of keeping an eye on the long-term trend, share a couple of industry secrets and focus you on some big-picture items to *always* keep in mind.

Looking at Where the Stock Market Entry Routes Are

Three routes into the stock market exist. Traditionally, you could either hold collective funds or buy shares in individual companies. Now there's a third way into longer-term investing – the exchange-traded fund or ETF (see the later section 'The advantages of exchange-traded funds' for more). And, of course, no rule prevents you travelling two or three of these routes at the same time.

With collective funds you have fees to pay. Here a company takes money from many small investors, pools it to give buying power and then entrusts it to a manager who decides what to buy and sell. Fund managers earn fees for this service. The main collective fund categories are investment and unit trusts (most are now officially renamed as open-ended investment companies or OEICs).

The advantage of having your own shares is that you're in control, and you don't have to pay yourself an annual fee for looking after them. Don't forget that although 1.5 per cent a year may not sound much, it adds up to a big sum over 10 to 20 years. This is especially true for pension funds, where some people can invest for 40 years or even more.

You can also consider passive investment (see the later section 'The passive versus active path to profits'), where you simply choose a vehicle such as UK or US stocks and then buy into a package of shares that reflect the indexes for these markets. You can do this via a collective fund or an ETF.

Identifying Two Top Investment Trade Tricks

In this section I let you in on two stock-market secrets. The first one, which is about the benefits of the passive-investment path to profits, is actually just classified material, so it's really not super secret. But the second one, which is about the benefits of exchange-traded funds, is top secret and for your eyes only, requiring the highest degree of confidentiality.

The passive versus active path to profits

One stock-market secret is that the long-term investor can do well by buying all the shares in companies that appear in an index such as Footsie, the Eurostoxx or the US's Standard & Poor's. Naturally, you'd do better if you could just spot the best 10 per cent. Try, though, and there's a big danger you'll get the worst 10 per cent!

 You can't buy all the shares in an index yourself unless you're very wealthy and prepared to monitor your holdings constantly. You need a specialist fund (backed by a well-programmed computer) to do this for you. Specialist fund types include index trackers and exchange-traded funds.

Buying all the shares of companies in an index in their same proportions as the index compilers use, irrespective of what anyone may think about their individual prospects, is called *passive investment*. Footsie trackers are popular. A *tracker* is a fund that aims to replicate the ups and downs of an index (here the FTSE 100 or Footsie) by buying all the constituent shares.

The opposite approach is called *active investment*, where you take a view on each company and only buy those that you think will do best. The problem is, as mentioned at the beginning of this section, you may end up buying the worst 10 per cent and losing a great deal of money!

Active versus passive investment is a very big debate. Most of the material published tends to come from those with prior positions and commercial interests on either side, so it tends to develop more heat than light. This dispute goes on whatever is happening to stock markets. Funds can only make money when the shares they invest in go up.

The pros of the passive approach

Here are the benefits of the passive-investment approach:

- ✔ The only thinking you need to do is deciding which index to follow, when to buy and ultimately when to sell.

- ✔ The computer works out which shares to buy and in what proportions.

- ✔ No index has ever gone down all the way to zero, so you'll never lose all your money. Bust and failing companies come out of indexes and are replaced by the shares of healthier firms.

- ✔ Following the ups and downs is easy. The index is published in newspapers and online.

- ✔ You're not wasting money on analysts and researchers, who often contradict each other. When some are saying sell and some are hollering buy, they can't all be right, can they?

- ✔ The charges are usually lower than other forms of investment. The typical tracker charges 0.3 to 0.5 per cent a year in management fees. Anything more is pure robbery because you're not getting any extra value. But active funds hit you for 1.5 per cent and sometimes more. All those yearly 0.5 to 1 per cent reductions in annual management charges plus lower entry costs add up to a big amount of money over 10 to 20 years.

- ✔ Over long periods, tracker funds usually come in at around the 35th to 40th percentile in fund performance tables. A percentile is a one-hundredth of the table, so in a table of 500 funds, each percentile would be five funds deep. A third of the way down would be the 33rd percentile; halfway is the 50th percentile. This means, trackers come somewhere just outside the top third in performance tables. Few active funds manage this on a consistent basis, and many never succeed in getting into the top third.

✔ You can use passivity for a *core and satellite* approach to investing. The passive fund is the core for your holdings, so you put 80 per cent or so of your money there. The satellites are your other holdings, where you back your hunches.

The pros of the active approach

Here are the benefits of the active-investment approach:

✔ You don't get landed with dud stocks. Index trackers have to keep failing shares heading to the knacker's yard until they're expelled from the index.

✔ You can buy into shares when they're still cheap or little known. The way indexes usually work is that companies are put on the list only when their value reaches a certain level, which may be too late for growth.

✔ You're not forced to change your portfolio just because an index compiler says to do so.

✔ You can pick defensive shares that will do better in falling markets and go for aggressive stocks in rising markets.

✔ You can buy shares in the proportion you want. You don't get landed with too many or too few in any particular company.

✔ You can avoid shares in dodgy or unethical industries, or if you really want to, you can opt instead for a basket of sin stocks, such as stocks from gambling, tobacco and armaments companies.

✔ You can pick shares to suit the level of dividend income you want to generate.

✔ You don't waste money in tracking error. Tracking error comes from all the costs a fund hits its customers with and the expenses it has to lay out. It also comes from being unable to replicate each movement in the underlying shares at precisely the right moment.

✔ Some indexes, such as the Japanese Nikkei, are difficult to track.

The advantages of exchange-traded funds

The usual route into the tracker concept is via a unit trust. And there are also a handful of investment trusts that track an index. But here's another stock-market secret for you: check out the exchange-traded fund or ETF. It's so hidden that most professional financial advisers don't know about it. Still, maybe they don't want to know. The commission-earning possibilities are even less than with tracker funds.

Why look at ETFs? The problem is, both unit trusts and investment trusts have drawbacks as trackers. For example, most unit trusts only allow dealing once or, at most, twice a day and at times to suit the managers. So that's not much use if you spot a sudden buying chance. An index can move 3 per cent or more within a day. That's a lot of money if you get the wrong side of it.

Both investment and unit trusts have a further disadvantage. Every time you buy into the fund, you have to pay stamp duty one way or another. (It's more hidden in a unit-trust purchase, but it's there all the same.)

The answer to these difficulties is something called an *exchange-traded fund (ETF)*. You buy this type of fund through a stockbroker just like any other share. But unlike other shares, an exchange-traded fund doesn't give you a stake in a company. The ETF is a sort of artificial stock-market creation, a piece of financial engineering from the guys who would be rocket scientists if they weren't so keen on money-making. Here the rocket science is called 'derivative trading'. And how this works would fill this book and a half, believe me (oh, and that's genuine understatement!).

But what the ETF does is dead simple. The ETF does what it says on the tin. For example, the Footsie ETF would move up and down exactly in line with the Footsie index, second by second, tenth of a point by tenth of a point. It's always spot on. And you can get regular dividend payments just as with a normal tracker fund.

You can save money as well. Derivatives don't attract UK government stamp duty, which takes 0.5 per cent up front from your other shares investment money. Otherwise, charges are similar to those imposed at the low end of the unit-trust trackers' fee range.

 You can use derivatives for all sorts of complicated strategies. The easiest is *shorting*, meaning that you can sell the ETF if you think the index is due to fall and then buy it back later at a lower price. The gap between the two is your profit or loss.

 Investment banks create ETFs. Banks can go bust. The danger always exists, even though tiny, that the bank may not be able to meet its liabilities.

 Check on the fund's costs before buying – anything over 0.5 per cent a year should ring alarm bells. And always check on the names of the manager, trustee and custodian. Do these ring true and do you know who they are, or is the ETF run by a group of 20-year-olds in the back streets of a Latin American shanty town?

Knowing What to Consider When Buying Individual Shares

You need to know this fact up front: you can buy great shares that slump and equities in crummy companies that go up. In other words, stock markets are fickle creatures that have no permanent rules.

When you play or watch football, you know that there are two halves and that each, ignoring injury time, should last for 45 minutes. You know what the object of the game is, and at the end, each team has a result, win, draw or lose.

Stock markets are different. In particular, there are no fixed timeframes and no clear goals. Shares go on until a company ceases to exist. This could be tomorrow or in a hundred years' time. Quality will carry the day eventually, but no one knows when that *eventually* will be or even whether the company will change directions for the better or worse in the meantime.

What you have to do is look at the big-picture items, such as the economy or interest rates, which have the power to push the great to mediocrity (or worse) or the very average to a nice little earner. And you have to keep in mind that markets swing very easily between feast and famine.

Knowing the psychological impact of the economy

How do you feel when you get out of bed in the morning? Do you feel (Mondays not counted) confident of your job or your pension; that you can make ends meet; that you can cope with the credit card bills; and that the mortgage isn't overwhelming? Or do you worry about your job; fear for your pension payments; fret about being able to afford a holiday this year; know your credit card is ruining you; and have no idea how you're going to pay the mortgage this month?

The likelihood, of course, is that you're somewhere between the euphoria of the first description and the misery of the second. But wherever you are on the scale of being happy or sad about your money prospects, the reason is likely because of the economy. People who prosper in good times have problems when the economy turns sour, even though they continue to work as hard and budget in the same way.

Investor psychology drives markets. When most people are happy, they have the confidence to buy shares, so shares go up in value.

Knowing the power of interest rates

The most important single factor in the modern economy is the interest rate. In the UK, the base rate (which sets the tone for all other interest rates) is fixed at noon on the first Thursday of each month by the Bank of England. This base rate dictates the interest level at which banks and very large companies can borrow money. In turn, it gives the cue to banks, building societies and loan companies in calculating the interest levels they charge to consumers for credit in stores, homebuyers for mortgages and smaller firms for the finance their businesses need. Everyone else pays more than the base rate, of course. Over the course of the 2008–2009 financial crisis, official interest rates collapsed to an all-time low of 0.5 per cent.

Interest rates also set the tone for share prices because:

✔ **Most companies borrow.** Finance directors calculate that borrowing is fine if the company can use that cash to produce a greater return than the interest bill. Suppose, for example, that a company borrows ₤1 million at 5 per cent per year. So the company will pay ₤50,000 in interest. It uses the money to buy a machine or open a new outlet that produces ₤70,000 per year in profits. The company is now ₤20,000 per year better off. If interest rates fall to 3 per cent, the cost of the bank loan falls to ₤30,000, so now the company gets ₤40,000 per year in profits. But what if interest rates rise to 10 per cent? The company is now spending ₤100,000 per year on the money borrowed, which produces ₤70,000. So it's losing money at the rate of ₤30,000 per year. Higher interest rates mean higher costs of borrowing. If you pay more to borrow the same amount of money, your profits will drop – and vice versa if interest rates fall.

Companies that borrow the most in relation to their size benefit the most from falling interest rates. This is called *gearing up*. Many now use the US term *leverage* instead.

✔ **Most individuals borrow to buy pricey consumer goods.** Companies have to sell products or services either directly to consumers or to other concerns who provide items for stores and services that deal with the ultimate consumer. When interest rates fall, consumers have more money in their pockets (called *disposable income* by economists) because they don't need to spend as much on mortgages and credit card loan costs. If rates rise, shoppers have less scope to buy goods. So higher interest rates dissuade people from borrowing, so fewer goods are sold and companies make lower profits. This is all bad for shares.

✔ **Company payouts look better when interest rates fall.** Say that you bought a share for ₤1 that (ignoring tax) pays 5p a year in dividends. At the time you bought, a cash account paid 5 per cent, or 5p, for every ₤1. Now, say that interest rates drop to 4 per cent. The dividend stays at 5 per cent, but the cash account rate falls to 4 per cent. Share dividends are now more attractive, so investors will buy the shares themselves, pushing up the price.

> ✔ **Falling interest rates mean the next time a company needs money, it won't have to pay the bank so much.** Therefore, it will be able to carry out its expansion, making the firm bigger and more valuable.

That said, interest rates are a blunt instrument, and they hit companies in different ways.

Here's a list of sectors that are bludgeoned the most by rising rates and that get top benefits from falling rates:

- ✔ **House builders.** They're usually big borrowers in comparison to their size. What they build is nearly always sold to consumers who need loans.

- ✔ **Retailers.** When rates rise, their customers have less cash because they're paying more for mortgages. Consumers are less likely to use credit cards. Most big purchases are non-essential and can be put off. But for how long? The new three-piece suite can nearly always wait; the new generation videocam is far from necessary; and the replacement fridge can stay on hold for longer.

- ✔ **Fund managers and life-insurance companies.** Firms that make their living out of the stock market hate rising interest rates, which scare people off equities. Customers put new money into savings accounts, so the fees these people get from investing other people's money fall.

- ✔ **Exporters.** Higher interest rates can often push up the value of your currency on foreign exchange markets. This is bad for exporters who get less when their foreign earnings are turned back into their home currency.

- ✔ **Banks.** Surprisingly perhaps, banks do badly when interest rates go up. They do charge more for loans, but not as many people want to borrow. Worse, banks can't hit customers with as big a gap (technically known as the *margin*) between what they give to savers and the amount they charge to borrowers.

And here are some stock-market areas that should do better than average when rates are rising:

- ✔ **Food retailers.** People have to eat! In tough times, people need a few shopping-therapy-style treats which are more likely to be a bottle of wine or a box of chocolates than new clothes or electronic goodies.

✔ **Discount shops.** Stores where nothing costs more than £1 or where you can buy a complete outfit with change from £50 are obvious winners in hard times.

✔ **Companies with cash.** Not all companies borrow. Some have big balances at the bank, so they profit if rates rise.

✔ **Tobacco companies and breweries.** People tend to smoke and drink more when they're miserable, whatever the health effects. And because they spend little on product development, these companies tend not to borrow and have lots of cash.

✔ **Importers.** Higher rates can mean a stronger currency so importers can buy their goods overseas with a smaller amount of their home currency.

Enjoying the Payments and Perks of Owning Shares

Shareholding has its plus points including, in some cases, the chance to pick up a bargain when you go shopping or away for a break. These plus points can lighten the down moments and help your finances when the shares themselves are looking miserable.

Getting dividends

Most companies send you a twice-a-year share payment (occasionally four times a year), called a *dividend*. It's the various companies' way of saying thank you for your cash and loyalty in hanging in there through thick and thin.

The first dividend of the year is called the *interim payment*, and the second is called the *final payment*. Sometimes, though, the final dividend is called the *second interim*. The company usually announces the interim payment with the six-monthly figures halfway through the firm's financial year, and announces the final dividend with the *preliminary results*, or *prelims*, of the financial year, so called because they're revealed before the official annual report. Some companies now pay out four times a year – these are usually those based overseas or those that have a large slice of their interests outside the UK.

Shareholders get to vote on the amount that the company will pay out as a final dividend for the year at the annual general meeting, although you can count the instances of investors turning down money on the fingers of one hand. This usually happens as a form of protest against either the company itself, an activity of that company or some of the directors.

When the company announces a dividend, it sets a date on which it'll pay the dividend to those on the shareholder register at that time. Investors who buy from that date onward must wait until the next time (probably in six months or so) for their first payment.

Most companies send a dividend cheque, even for a small amount. You could even end up with a cheque worth less than the stamp on the envelope used to send it. Most companies will also arrange for your dividend payment to be sent straight to your bank account.

Another option, offered by many big companies and virtually all funds, is *automatic dividend reinvestment* (sometimes called DRIP, for Dividend Re-Investment Plan). Your money is used to buy new shares in the company at the price ruling on the day the dividend is announced. Of course, it's unlikely that your dividend payment will buy an exact number of shares, so usually some change will be carried over to the next dividend payment and then added to your dividend.

Reinvesting dividends makes sense if you don't need to spend the money. Barclays Equity Gilt Study figures show that much of the advantage of shares is lost otherwise.

An investor with £10,000 at the end of 1979 would have shares worth £101,537 after 30 years, at the end of 2009 (ignoring costs and tax). Putting the dividends back into shares would've turned that same £10,000 into £250,772. Even making allowances for tax and costs, reinvesting dividends gives a huge, long-term uplift to your investments. It also has the advantage that you continue buying shares when prices are low so you can enjoy any eventual bounce upwards.

Getting discounts and freebies

A number of companies do more than pay out dividends. They want their investors to share in the company in a more tangible way through share perks. These companies give private investors a discount on the group's goods or services which vary from money off a new house to a promotional goody bag handed out at the annual general meeting.

Chapter 8

Analysing Stock-Market-Quoted Companies

. . . .

In This Chapter

▶ Understanding what company profits are all about

▶ Getting familiar with the price/earnings ratio

▶ Understanding that dividend declaration you get from the company

▶ Working through company takeovers

▶ Deciphering share price charts

. . . .

*B*eing a successful share investor involves looking at numbers and understanding them. But don't worry. You don't need a PhD in mathematics or rocket-science physics. Much of the figure work involves nothing more complicated than looking to see whether something is going up or down. And most of the rest involves the simple task of comparing figures from one company with those from another.

The most difficult maths task is working out percentage sums, which you can do on a calculator that costs less than £10, or you've probably got one on your phone for free. Many investment decisions depend on knowing how a figure compares with the previous year and with expectations of the future.

That's what this chapter is all about – being a successful share investor by looking at numbers from stock-market-quoted companies and then understanding what those numbers mean.

Of course, if you've decided you don't want to invest in individual shares but stick to collectives, then you could skip this chapter. But even if you leave it up to fund managers, it's still useful to know about these basic analysis tools.

Comparing Apples with Apples: The Gospel According to the Market

Stock markets don't have set rules or timescales like a game of football. So whatever figures you come up with during your investment number crunching, you must compare them with other numbers that are around at the same time.

For example, you may calculate or hear that profits at a company have increased by 10 per cent. Well, that's obviously better than profits going down – or even going up by just 9 per cent. But you can only see how important that 10 per cent gain is by referring to the market as a whole and to companies that compete with the company you're looking at.

If the market average gain is 15 per cent, your company is in house building and rival construction companies have gained 20 per cent, then your share is doing very badly! The converse also applies, of course. A 10 per cent profits advance when most other comparable firms are struggling to make any gains is really good news!

Identifying the Basic Building Blocks of Companies: Profits

Investors in shares have one concern that overrides all else. They need to know how much profit (or loss) the company will make in the future. Nothing else counts. The past is more than a foreign country; it's a nowhere place.

But future profits are the great unknown, although investors try to estimate what they'll be and how they'll compare with other companies. Share values adjust to these expectations, and investors then compare their hopes or fears with the reality when it's announced.

When stock-market experts forecast a 20 per cent profits increase at a company, they factor that expectation into the share price. They calculate whether 20 per cent is above, below or in line with competitor companies and with the market as a whole. They also look to see how that compares with previous figures and expectations from the company. And outside the direct orbit of these experts and the firms they work for, other market participants also consider the forecasters' credibility. A forecast from an analyst known to have a good record and close contacts with the company counts for more than a forecast from a largely unknown source.

But the real test is the actual profit number when it's officially released by the company. If the reality is 30 per cent, the share price will gain on the news. But if the gain fails to reach 20 per cent or only scrapes by that figure, disappointed investors will sell, so the shares may fall unless some other positive news emerges. Targets in the stock market are there to beat, not just to equal. Otherwise, it's 'all in the price' – a phrase meaning investors have weighed up what the expectations were and have adjusted the share value accordingly.

Examining a company's profit and loss account

Look at a company's annual report and its profit and loss (known as the *p & l*) account. It lists lots of different sorts of profit. You need to find the right one to see whether the company is going forward or backward, but you also need to understand the others to see the message they give out.

 Most company accounts are called *consolidated* because they bring together all the various subsidiaries that big firms have. You can ignore any other profit and loss accounts, although if you want to see them you can find them at Companies House and you can pay for a copy if you want. You really don't need to.

All UK companies have to produce detailed accounts once a year. Quoted concerns also issue half-yearly statements to show their progress. And a growing minority come up with figures every three months. In the US, quarterly reporting is the rule for most companies, so UK firms with substantial US interests tend to produce figures every three months. All these figures are the key to what's going on. Most sets of figures in the UK follow an established pattern, which starts with the biggest number at the top of the page and keeps taking away the further down you go. So the top line may be billions, but the bottom may be pennies. (When you look at a company's account, note that accountants don't use minus signs. Instead, they use brackets to indicate items to subtract. Likewise, if a company makes a loss, the account shows that figure in brackets.)

Here's a breakdown of what you'll see on a sample company's account – from the top to the bottom with some figures and what they tell you. Note that most accounts show sums in millions. Note, too, that this stuff is technical, even though I'm not explaining the most complicated versions. The latter are really impossible to follow unless you have a postgraduate qualification in company accounts from oil and insurance companies.

- ✔ **Turnover (£100 million).** This is the very biggest figure. It lists the amount people spend with the company. For a high-street store, it's the amount that came in through the tills. For a bank, it largely consists of the income from interest on loans.

- ✔ **Cost of sales (£80 million).** This is the amount the company has spent on raw materials as well as manufactured items it has bought to sell to customers.

- ✔ **Gross profit (£20 million).** This is what's left after taking the cost of sales away from the sales themselves. It's the biggest profit figure, but there's a lot to take away from it.

- ✔ **Operating expenses (£15 million).** This is the cost of running the company, including staff salaries and rent on premises. The pay that directors get is listed in notes to the accounts, the small print where quite a bit of the detail is hidden.

- ✔ **Operating profit (£5 million).** This is what the company would make if it operated in a vacuum! If there were no tax to pay or interest on bank loans to count, this would be the actual profit. It's a good indicator of a company's management efficiency. If two competitor firms both sell £100 million, the one with an operating profit of £5 million is running itself better than the one with an operating profit of £4 million.

✔ **Exceptional items ($500,000).** These are one-off items that really have nothing to do with the day-to-day running of the business – things like profits made from selling off a piece of spare land or the expenses of relocating the firm. They can be positive or negative. Firms often don't have any of these items.

✔ **Profit on ordinary activities before interest ($4.5 million).** This tells you how much the company made before paying for bank loans. It's a useful indicator of progress because it doesn't involve a major external such as interest, over which the company itself has no control whatsoever. Don't worry. This section is a fair way along the road but there's still an accounting hurdle or two to go.

✔ **Net interest payable ($500,000).** This is the cost of bank and other loans needed to run the business less any interest earned on bank deposits. Occasionally, companies may have earned more interest than they spent. This is an important figure because it tells you how susceptible the company is to interest-rate changes. Here, the interest charge is 10 per cent of the operating profit. Compare this with previous years and with competitor firms.

✔ **Profit before tax ($4 million).** This is the big headline figure and the profit definition used in most media reports.

✔ **Tax ($400,000).** Everyone has to pay taxes, but companies have ways and means of keeping the figure low.

✔ **Profit after tax ($3.6 million).** This is the amount the company has for ploughing back into the business and for paying out dividends. This amount is entirely at the control of the directors.

✔ **Minority interests and preference dividends ($200,000).** These are amounts companies must pay to special groups of investors before paying their own shareholders. Many companies don't have this item.

✔ **Profit attributable to ordinary shareholders ($3.4 million).** This is what you and all the other equity holders have to share out.

✔ **Dividends ($1.9 million).** This is the cost of the payments made to shareholders.

✔ **Retained profit for the year ($1 million).** This is what's left to plough back into the company for future expansion.

✔ **Earnings per share (17p).** This is the profit attributable to ordinary shareholders (£3.4m) divided by the number of shares in issue – in this case 20 million. It comes at the end, but it's a key figure for working out how well your investment is doing.

Understanding what company profits and losses actually mean

The ideal scenario is for a company to make record profit gains every year and beat the expectations of the experts by a huge margin. Don't ever bank on this happening, though. If such a paragon of virtue company existed, its shares would be really expensive because such amazing expectations would already have been 'discounted by the market' (that's another way of saying 'it's all in the price').

The 99.99 per cent probability is that the companies whose shares you buy will have a variable profits record, doing better in some periods than in others. Your job is to understand what the figures mean.

Profits may not always be quite as real or as rosy as a company's investor and media relations teams like to make out. And although no one wants to make a loss, getting into the red may not always be a disaster or even a danger signal.

So headline profit figures may not be what they seem. Following are some key profit moves to look for and assess. And don't forget that many companies are great at creative accounting, which is the stock-market equivalent of turning a sow's ear into a silk purse. Creative accounting, or window dressing, can go too far, as in the cases of Enron, Lehman Brothers or the downright fraudulent Ponzi scheme from jailed fund chief Bernie Madoff. Here are some examples of creative accounting to watch out for:

✔ **Rising profits year on year.** These sound really good. In most cases, they are. These are just the sort of companies investors love. But look out for comparisons with rival companies that may be doing even better; whether the company is doing anything more than just keeping up with rising prices in its product area; tricks such as massaging the profits upward with accounting devices; and whether the rising profits are due to the company buying other firms and incorporating their earnings into its own.

✔ **Profits reported each year but sometimes up and sometimes down.** This is a normal pattern, especially if firms can't rely on rising prices year after year to give paper profits. Check that the ups are as good if not better than competitor firms. Look at the reasons for the setbacks. Could they have been avoided? Did rivals do better? Did the company warn shareholders adequately that there might be problems?

✔ **Making neither a profit nor a loss.** Not a good sign, but if the company is in a healthy business with a good reputation, this status may say something about the failings of the management. Good companies with poor people at the top tend to end up with a takeover bid, good news for shareholders. Don't forget that breaking even when others are losing loads of cash *is* doing well. Check that directors aren't overpaying themselves.

✔ **Losing money.** Acceptable reasons include heavy research and development costs, a company starting up and needing to spend heavily before establishing itself, and economic slumps. Find out what the company is doing to turn itself around. If there's no reason or light at the end of the deficit tunnel, run a mile from this company. Don't forget, it's your money the company's losing, so there has to be some gain after your pain.

Published company figures are two to four months out of date when they're released. Circumstances by then may have changed. Companies take different times to add up the figures. High-street stores and banks tend to be quick. Firms with lots of different overseas offshoots and smaller companies are usually slower.

Bad figures take longer to add up than good ones. That's not literally true, but companies that delay releasing figures or are late compared with previous years are usually in financial trouble. Treat any postponement as a danger signal.

Knowing What to Look at First: Earnings Per Share

You may only have one share in a company that has issued one billion. But that *earnings per share (eps)* figure at the end of the company's profit and loss account is what you get. And even if it's at the very bottom of the page, it's where in-the-know investors look first.

You can use the eps figure rather than the headline profit to see whether the company is really moving ahead. It may have issued millions more shares to acquire other firms, which could result in the profit it brings in boosting the pre-tax profits figure, but once it's divided up among more shares, the end result could be down.

For example, say that Company A has £10 million profits attributable to shareholders who have 10 million shares between them. So each earns £1 per share. Then Company A buys Company B by issuing 10 million shares. Profits go up to £15 million, but each share now only has 75p in earnings because the £15 million must be divided out 20 million ways. The takeover has been bad (or to put it in jargon, *non-earning enhancing*). It might be better later on, of course. Or even worse. Owners of shares in companies that are bought tend to fare better than those who own shares in companies that are doing the acquiring.

The eps figure is also honest because it's after tax. It measures what's really yours and not a slice the taxman will grab.

What a price/earnings ratio is

The earnings per share figure lets you compare one year with the next at the same company. But it's pretty useless if you want to rate one firm against another. Whether your earnings are high or low all depends on the share price.

A 20p eps sounds twice as good as a 10p eps. But it's not necessarily so. It all depends on the share price. Dividing the earnings into the share price gives a magic figure called the *p/e*, which stands for *price/earnings ratio*, and it's widely used in working out whether a share is good value. It tells you how many years of earnings at the last published level you'd need to equal the share price.

Loss-making companies can't have a price/earnings ratio because they have no earnings. That's why the p/e column in newspaper listings sometimes shows a dash. Some investors calculate the loss/earnings ratio, and it can be useful to compare two loss-making companies.

If two companies have identical prospects, the one with the lower p/e number is the better deal. If both companies are going to earn, say, 10p per share, the one with the p/e of 12 equalling a 120p share price is more attractive than the share on a 15 times p/e because then you'll pay 150p for the same thing.

What a prospective price/earnings ratio tells you

The p/e is a great comparative tool. It's widely quoted in newspaper reports, and it's carried in many share listings both on- and offline. It goes up when share prices rise and down when they fall. But it has one big weakness. The figure you see is based on the most recent accounts, it's called the historical p/e and it's unlikely that the company is going to make the same profits again. It might make more or less.

The way around this weakness is the *prospective p/e*, which is based on what the stock market thinks the company is going to make in the current financial year and sometimes in the year or two after that. For example, a company with earnings last year of 10p and a current share price of 100p has a p/e of 10. The forecast is for earnings of 20p per share, so the prospective p/e falls to 5 (100p divided by 20p). If the forecast were for earnings of 4p per share, the prospective p/e would rise to 25.

Take prospective figures with a pinch of salt. They're educated guesses with a bit of help from the company itself, which steers or guides stockbroker analysts in the right direction. Some investors prefer consensus figures that average out the guesstimates of all the analysts who publish their work.

Beware of shares with astronomic price/earnings ratios that imply you'd have to wait 100 or more years to get your share price back if earnings stayed the same. Mega ratios usually come with shares with more hype than hope, more faith than a fair future. Or they may simply be figures based on a previous year when earnings were much higher.

Knowing What Dividends Really Mean

Would you like a twice-per-year cheque from your share investments that you can spend or save or plough back into the stock market? Or are you happy to just rely on whatever your shares fetch on the day you decide to sell? Most UK investors opt for the first choice.

Companies pay out *dividends*, or share payments, usually around every six months, some quarterly, of so many pence per share. That price is multiplied by the number of shares you have, so you're sent a cheque or a bank transfer for the amount to the nearest penny.

Some companies offer reinvestment schemes, so you can use your dividend to buy more shares. Because your dividend probably won't buy an exact number of shares, any leftover amount is carried over to the next dividend payment. (You can only buy whole shares, unlike units in unit-trust funds, which subdivide each unit by 100.)

Dividends represent your share of the profits. And they're a major part of the UK share scene. But not all companies are expected to pay dividends. Exceptions are new companies, where investors expect all the profits to be ploughed into the business, as well as companies making losses, which can't afford to spare the cash. However, when companies are in the position where they can afford the payments, they're expected to do so. Holding back without an explanation is viewed with grave suspicion and a fast-falling share price!

Understanding what dividends tell about the company

Because the dividend is seen as a vital part of the share make-up in the UK (less so in many other countries), analysts look at its level as a vital sign of that firm's financial health or perhaps lack of health.

The essential figure is the *dividend yield*, a figure that requires all the dividends in a year to be added up. Some firms pay more than twice a year, and payments are rarely equal. Companies with seasonal businesses, such as package holiday firms, may pay only a token amount at one payment and nearly everything in the other payout. That's because the cash flowing in and out of the company is uneven.

Dividends and dividend yields are based on the past. These may not provide any indication of the future. For instance, the dividend yield in a company that's failing could look very attractive. But there'd be a strong likelihood of a dividend cut (or getting rid of it altogether), so the yield here would be fictional.

The price/earnings ratio rises with share prices. But the dividend as a ratio falls when shares go up.

Looking at dividends, like everything else in the investment world, is comparison work. No absolute levels exist. For example, many companies that paid a 10 per cent dividend yield in the inflationary 1970s and 1980s went down to 2 per cent by the end of the 1990s.

You need to be concerned with two dividend yield figures. The current rate is the one you use for analysis. But the rate worked out for the price you paid for the share can also be important because it gives you an idea of what another investment would need to produce to give you the same amount of spendable cash. If the current share price at 300p offers you a 10 per cent yield, you'd have a 30 per cent yield on your cash if you bought the shares at 100p.

To look at dividends, you need benchmarks:

✔ **The average yield on the FTSE All Share Index.** See whether your share comes up with a higher or lower number. The higher the figure, the less the stock market thinks of the share's future growth prospects. Many newspapers and websites carry this statistic.

✔ **The sector average.** This looks at companies in similar businesses to your own, such as breweries or software companies. This figure is also published in some newspapers and is available online.

✔ **The yield on a basket of UK government stocks, or** *gilts.* This helps tell you what you'd get for your money in the safest UK investment. If the dividend yield is lower than the one for gilts, you'll have to hope for future growth from the share to compensate. Otherwise, there's no point in taking the risk of equity purchase. This is called the *equity risk premium.*

Deciphering the signs that dividends provide

Comparing a dividend yield or return with its benchmark, such as a sector average, and the amount paid in previous years gives a list of possibilities for investors looking for pointers to a company's future health. All the ideas here offer clues to the company and how other investors see it.

Rising dividend payments

Rising dividend payments are what investors expect. The ideal share gives a bit extra each time to reflect growing profits.

But investors would be worried if payments went up faster than earnings because it would show that the company isn't investing in its own future. Instead, it's trying to buy stock-market favour, perhaps to ward off an expected takeover bid. The exception is when a company has a lot of cash and has announced that it thinks shareholders can make better use of it than the company management. You could get a *special dividend* – a one-off return of cash that won't be replicated in the future.

Static dividend payments

Generally, static dividend payments are viewed as bad news because the company isn't growing its profits. Static dividend payments are viewed as even worse news if the company has to dip into its bank account to pay the dividend. Firms shouldn't borrow to pay dividends. Doing this is generally seen as a danger signal.

Falling or no dividend payments

Falling dividend payments or no dividend payments are really bad news, but companies often prepare investors for this situation ahead of the announcement because it's even worse if the decision to reduce or cut out payments comes as a surprise.

As a rule, a company that says it's being forced to halve its dividend will see its share price fall by roughly the same amount over a relatively short period. Investors are more forgiving if they can see light at the end of this tunnel in the shape of a return to dividend growth in the future.

Very high dividend payments

When you see very high dividends, do a reality check. Can this continue? Or is it an attempt to buy investor favour?

Dividend yields shown in newspapers are historic because they're based on the most recent payouts. The company may have announced a reduction or complete cancellation of its next dividend, so check websites and other news sources before relying on this yield figure.

Even if nothing has been said publicly, investors can often put two and two together and find out whether a company is going to have to cut dividends. If the company is about to cut or abandon (technically called *passing*) the dividend, then investors tend to sell.

Looking at the dividend cover

Dividing the dividend per share into the earnings per share gives something called the *cover*. For example, an earnings per share of 20p with a dividend of 5p gives a four times cover.

This figure is the number of times the dividend could've been paid out from after-tax earnings. In this case, the 5p dividend could've been paid four times over, so the cover number is four.

Too low a number, especially less than one, tells you the company is pulling out all the stops and all the cash from wherever it can to avoid the indignity of a dividend cut. Companies can only get away with this if they have a really good excuse and a promise that they'll go back to a higher cover in the future.

There's also the danger of running near to empty. A company paying out most or all of its earnings in dividends has nothing to fall back on if times become harder and profits fall.

But too high a cover, perhaps more than four or five times, suggests that the company is hoarding cash. Nothing's wrong if you can see the reason, so find out whether its research, development and other expansion requirements really need it to be quite so mean to shareholders.

Looking at Takeovers: Good, Bad, or Ugly?

Takeovers occur when one company wants to buy another stock-market-quoted company lock, stock and barrel.

They get headlines that can be emotive, as a foreign company bids for a 'much loved, iconic company', or exciting, as when a bid battle occurs with rival companies bidding auction-style for the target.

Whatever the reaction, takeovers involve all shareholders because whatever the company directors recommend the real power lies with those owning the equity.

Takeovers happen because:

 ✔ The company making the acquisition thinks it can squeeze more profits out of the target company, and so it's worth paying for.

✔ The target company has profitable patents or products that the acquiring company wants.

✔ The target company is a rival, and a successful takeover bid would mean less competition. (Note that this scenario may have to pass UK Competition Commission hurdles if the result would place too much power into the hands of one company.)

✔ The target company has lots of assets, such as property, that can be bought for less than their true worth and then sold for a profit – a practice known as *asset stripping*. It's frowned upon, but it still happens.

✔ The acquiring company is running out of steam and ideas, so it wants to bring in a smaller, more successful firm to rejuvenate it. This scenario is sometimes called a *reverse takeover* because the smaller firm ends up in charge.

Whatever the reason for them, takeovers usually generate big share price gains for the target company. Takeovers are supposed to be top secret before the company makes an official announcement, but leaks and rumours are common even though they're supposed to be covered by legislation banning insider trading.

At least ten takeover rumours exist for every real bid. So don't believe every one you see mentioned in newspapers and elsewhere.

The share price of the target company goes up for the usual reason of supply and demand. In this case, there's demand for every share from the bidder, so the value naturally goes up.

The company making the bid hopes that the directors of the target company will recommend the bid to their own shareholders. But the shareholders want to see a second bidder, counter-bidder or rejection from the target company because it should send the price up even further. Investors with shares in the target company always benefit from an auction between two or more determined bidders.

Holders in the target company may be offered cash or shares (or a mix of the two) in the acquiring company. Cash is the best option because you know what you're getting; shares will go up and down. A loan stock option, which is a special device where the company keeps your takeover cash and pays you regular interest on the amount, may also be offered. The purpose is to help investors cut down on capital gains tax bills. They do this by cashing their loan options in instalments each year rather than the whole lot in one go.

Takeovers are mostly good for shareholders in the target companies. Many academic studies show that takeovers are less good for acquiring firms. It's common for shares in the bidding firm to fall when it announces a takeover.

Discussing Technical Analysis: The Arcane World of Share Price Charts

Warning here: what I discuss in this section is so technical that it's called *technical analysis*. It involves looking at share price charts to make decisions rather than other factors such as earnings expectations or the future of the market where the firm operates. Cynics say technical analysts, or *chartists*, can make decisions without even knowing what business the firm's in. So technical analysis isn't everyone's cup of tea. But those who use it swear by it, and fans include a number of stock-market movers and shakers.

It's a way of making investment decisions that goes in and out of fashion. So you need to know about technical analysis even if you dismiss it as mumbo-jumbo.

Most people look at the fundamentals of shares. The fundamentals include the general economic situation, industry-specific trends, interest rates and foreign currency exchange rates, how the company you're looking at is seen to be doing, balance sheet strengths and weaknesses, the company's products, the company's management, and a host of other financial and business factors.

But a minority of investors reckon that looking at the fundamentals is a waste of time. So these investors go back to basics – so far back that some don't even care what the name is of the share, bond, currency or commodity they're looking at. Instead, they revert to one of the very early lessons investors have to take in. And that lesson is that you can't always explain what's going on except by saying that prices rise when buyers outnumber sellers and that prices go down when sellers outnumber buyers. So instead of looking at fundamental factors, they do technical analysis: draw up charts of prices, log the ups and downs and look for patterns. It's the ultimate version of supply and demand.

The theory of technical analysis is that markets move on expectations and sentiment rather than cold facts. Fans of price charts say that facts are usually known and taken into the price, but you need the *psychology* of market participants to get a real picture. And the only way you can get this psychology is via a chart showing the forces of buying and selling. Technical analysts believe that price charts show human emotions present in investors – emotions such as greed and fear, panic and elation – and that facts are often manipulated to suit these emotions. So when greed rules, all the fundamentals become positive.

Share price chart fans say they can often spot big movements before they happen by picking up unusual patterns. They say they can see through the 'noise' coming from companies, including attempts to make bad events look good, and that they don't need to read company statements or work out whether a denial of a story such as a takeover bid is true or not.

Technical analysts, or *chartists*, produce all sorts of patterns. Some charts cover a very brief time, and others look at decades. It's an attempt to read the future by evaluating the past. Here are some patterns and what they mean:

- ✔ **The moving average:** This is a line that smoothes out short-term fluctuations by averaging prices over the past (usually 100 or 200 trading days). The trick is to compare this line with the actual day-to-day ups and downs. The idea is to see whether the longer-term trend is moving up or down.

- ✔ **New highs and new lows:** This is not a chart at all, but a list based on new tops and bottoms for a share over a period, usually a year. Some newspapers print the number of shares that have made new high or new low points for the year. They may also print their names.

As the numbers of new highs or new lows increase, the likelihood is that prices are due to reverse. This isn't surprising. At the very top of a share market with lots of new highs, there's a panic to get in, so share values zoom up. At the bottom of a falling market with lots of new lows, there's a rush to get out, so a record number of shares hit new bottoms.

✔ **Head and shoulders:** This is one of many body-part patterns used in share price charts. The first shoulder is formed by a line as the price is ticking along. Then the line shoots up to form the top of the head as the price increases. If the line then comes down to form a new shoulder, the outlook is poor because the price has decreased. Chartists reckon that the head represents excitement from buyers, which has now ended.

✔ **Reverse head and shoulders:** This is the head-and-shoulders pattern turned upside down. If the head-and-shoulders pattern points to lower prices, then a reverse head and shoulders must look to better values.

✔ **Double bottom:** This is not a body part pattern! If a share hits a low point twice in a period, but the second low point is not as bad as the first, then chartists take it as a positive sign.

✔ **Double top:** This is the opposite of the double-bottom pattern and hence a bad sign. Nothing to do with darts.

✔ **Support level:** Chartists use a variety of statistical methods to put a line on the chart that shows where buyers are likely to come in. This level can put a floor under the share price. But it's not solid and recalculating the support level can create a new floor.

✔ **Resistance level:** This shows where sellers are likely to overpower buyers, so when a price reaches this level it's likely to go no further and will probably succumb to selling pressure. It's a ceiling, but just like the support level, it's not set in stone.

Chapter 9

Banking on Bonds

· ·

· ·

During the 1970s, 1980s and most of the 1990s, bonds were boring. Worse, they were guaranteed losers. They were no-hope purchases for no-hope purchasers. The only sensible investments during this time were equities. Shares in quoted companies made real gains even after the high inflation of much of this period. Even mediocre shares in boring companies earned their keep. It all had to do with something called the cult of the equity. Pension-fund managers, who controlled more and more of the stock market during the second half of the 20th century, bought shares with their members' money. Their counterparts in the United States and Europe continued to buy bonds, but their performance didn't compare with that of the UK management firms. Equities ruled.

But then something strange happened that caught all the equity folks by surprise, even though they should've seen it a million miles off. The members of those pension funds got older and the number of new employees joining fell dramatically as scheme after scheme was closed to new entrants. Fund managers no longer had to deal with a collection of 30-somethings who didn't worry much about pensions, but a large number of retired or almost retired folks. Their customers needed secure pension payments each month. And the only way they could get those monthly payments with any degree of security was through bonds. Shares, with their big ups and downs, just aren't suited to regular pay cheques.

Over the past ten years or so, bonds have come full circle. They were out of fashion when equities boomed, came back in fashion when equities slumped and just when they reached the top of the popularity charts, equities or shares came back into favour again. But with an ageing population looking for some security for life savings, bond salespeople, bond issuers, bond purchasers and bond traders aren't likely to find themselves on the redundancy scrapheap anytime soon. Leaving aside whether they can beat equities or property or not, bonds do have a role. And even if you don't want to buy bonds, you need to know about them because their prices can determine other parts of the financial mix.

This chapter gives you the savvy about bonds so that you, too, can be a fashionable investor.

Getting Down to the Bottom Line on Bonds

Bond is one of those words that the financial services industry uses all over the place. Industry folks like it because it inspires confidence. In this chapter, though, I'm referring to the technical meaning of the word. At its basic level, a *bond* is a loan made by investors to a company, national government or international body. In return, the company, government or international body offers to pay the holder a set sum of interest on set dates and promises to repay a pre-established amount on a set date in the future. Because of all this certainty, bonds are often called *fixed-interest* or *fixed-income investments*.

Cash is the lowest-risk investment idea around. Bonds are one step up from the security of cash in an established bank. The returns are a little higher, but you have to take a little more risk on board for the privilege. Of course, I'm talking about real bonds issued by genuine governments and classy companies here – not the highly complex 'bonds' sold by financial advisers, which are based on some very tricky financial engineering. Some of these, known as 'precipice bonds', lost investors all their cash, costing them huge amounts when their cash fell over a cliff edge.

In some ways, bonds are like cash. Here's the simplest bond deal: a company needs money, and you lend it £10,000. It promises to pay you 5 per cent interest (£500 a year) divided into six-monthly instalments, so you get £250 (less tax) twice a year. The company also promises to repay your £10,000 on a fixed future date – say 31 January 2020.

This sounds very much like a fixed-rate mortgage where you promise to pay a set sum of interest at regular intervals and repay the capital borrowed sometime in the future at a date laid down in the home-loan paperwork. For the company borrowing the money, that's a true assessment.

But for the investor, bonds have one big extra dimension over the bank-style loan. Bonds are traded on stock markets. Although the cost to issuers, such as companies or governments, doesn't change during the bond's life, the value to the holder can change all the time. The price goes up and down with economic variables, most importantly interest rates. But the amount the company has to pay when the bond reaches its payback, or maturity, date doesn't vary (except for a few index-linked bonds – bonds whose values mirror rising prices).

If the certificate says £10,000 (known as the *nominal amount*), then £10,000 is what the holder gets back on maturity, regardless of the price that person paid. I consider what the bond is worth between your purchase and its final maturity (or redemption) date in 'Identifying what makes bond prices go up and down', later in this chapter.

'Do I need bonds?'

You need bonds if you think they'll outperform equities and other investments, such as property or cash. But you also need them if

- ✔ You're a cautious investor who wouldn't be happy with share price ups and downs.

- ✔ You have a defined aim for your money, such as you must pay education fees on fixed dates or you want to give a set sum to a child on graduation or reaching a certain age.

✔ You have investment funds for your retirement years, and you're within five to ten years of stopping work. Some plans allow you to move gradually into bonds from shares. This arrangement, known as *lifestyling*, helps prevent your pension from being hit by a sudden fall in share values.

✔ You've retired and need certainty of income from your savings.

'Tell me the big differences between bonds and shares'

Companies that need to raise cash can issue equities – or *shares* as they're better known. They can also issue bonds (called *corporate bonds* to differentiate them from those put out by governments) and get the same amount. So what's the difference?

✔ Shares are permanent. Once issued, they carry on until the company ceases to exist, either because it goes bust, is absorbed by another company or buys in its own shares to cancel them. Equally, investors have no time limit on their equity holdings (except for a few specialised investment trusts).

✔ Bonds usually (although a handful of exceptions exist) have a fixed life, which is shown on the paperwork you get. You know when they'll stop paying you a regular amount and give back the original cash instead.

✔ Shares pay dividends, which can go down as well as up. Sometimes dividend payments are missed altogether. The rate of dividend depends on the profits of the company and what it needs to do with the cash it generates.

✔ Bonds pay interest (known as the *coupon* because old bond certificates used to contain small squares that holders had to cut out every six months to claim the payment; from *couper*, the French word for *cut*). This interest is fixed whether the company is doing well or not. Bond interest must be paid before any share dividends are issued.

✔ Shares give holders a say in the company proportional to their holding. Shareholders are the legal owners of the company, and they get to attend an annual general meeting where they can quiz the board.

✔ Bondholders, in most circumstances, have no ownership or annual meeting voting rights. Bondholders are only active when the bond issuer (company or government) is in financial trouble.

✔ Share prices can be very volatile.

✔ Bond prices vary less from day to day.

✔ Shareholders have to worry about how well the company is doing. Share prices depend on profits.

✔ Bondholders have to worry more about credit risk – the chance that a company will do so badly that it'll default on loan repayment or on an interest payment. Some companies have different classes of bonds, some of which go to the front of the queue if the company goes bust.

Looking at UK Government Bonds: All That's Gilt Isn't Gold

Understanding the basics of bonds is easiest by looking at *gilts*, which are UK government bonds. In case you're interested, they're known as gilts or gilt-edged because the certificates used to have gold-coloured borders. That titbit aside, gilts are one of the ways the government pays for its spending other than by raising taxes. (It also borrows through National Savings.)

Gilts are super-safe. You don't have to worry about the issuing company going bust. Think about it: if the UK government fails to pay its legal obligations, then there'll be a lot more problems than just some angry investors!

Gilts also appeal to cautious UK investors because they're in sterling. You can buy bonds in dollars, euros or several other currencies, but you'll have to worry about currency exchange rate risks as well.

Gilts (and all other bonds) can go up and down in value. But the shorter the remaining life of a bond, the more you can be sure of it. Government bonds react to interest rates above all. If your bond has only a few months before redemption, there's not much chance of a big interest-rate change. If it has 20 years to go, then it's anyone's guess what will happen.

Identifying What Makes Bond Prices Go Up and Down

Put your £1,000 savings in the bank, and your money stays at £1,000. What you generally don't know, though, is how much interest you'll get. Most bank accounts have variable rates. Put the same money into a gilt or other bond, and your £1,000 could be worth more or less the next day. But you'll know how much interest you'll get. With a bond, your interest is fixed, but your capital value is variable.

Like everything else in stock markets, bond prices are driven by supply and demand. When people want to buy, the price rises. And vice versa.

Working out why people want to buy or sell shares is complicated. So many factors hit the average company that it's a real juggling act to get them all in the air and then make some sense out of them when they land. But bonds are simpler. Investors look at three main factors:

- ✔ Interest rates in the economy
- ✔ Credit risks or the chances of the bond issuer defaulting on obligations
- ✔ The remaining life of the bond

The interest-rate gamble

Investors buy bonds to provide interest payments. Purchasing bonds is only worthwhile if all the following points apply:

- ✔ The rate of interest together with any gain you make between the buying price and maturity is better than the rate you're likely to get from a bank or building society over the life of the bond. The interest rate has to be higher because of the uncertainty to your savings. Additionally, buying and selling a bond costs money in stockbroker fees.

✔ **You have confidence in the bond issuer.** Bonds can go bust. There's always the danger that the issuer will go bankrupt or have financial troubles that stop short of total disaster. This can happen with governments as well as companies. No government-backed rescue scheme exists if it all goes wrong. And even if you're happy about who you're lending your money to, the longer a bond has to run, the greater the chance that interest rates will change or something unforeseen will happen.

✔ **You know what will happen if you hold the bond to maturity.** You may receive more for your bond than you paid for it, so making a profit. Or you could receive less if you paid *over par* – more than £100 for each £100 on the certificate.

✔ **You're happy that inflation will be moderate or non-existent.** Rising prices will erode the real value of your savings. You'll get the face value of your bond on redemption even if the £100 of the future will only buy a small fraction of what it buys now.

Bonds offer fixed interest and a fixed repayment of the nominal capital on a future date. But although they're a lower-risk investment, they aren't risk free. Assuming everyone is happy about the quality of the bond issuer and its ability to hold to its side of the bargain, bonds are a balance between their capital value and the interest rate. When interest rates fall, bond prices go up. When interest rates rise, bond values fall. This scenario is like a seesaw, where both ends can't rise or fall at the same time.

When interest rates fall

Suppose that interest rates are 10 per cent and you buy a bond offering a 10 per cent coupon for £100. You get £5 twice a year, or £10 in all.

Now suppose that interest rates fall to 5 per cent. Bond values go up when interest rates fall, so the value of your bond to new investors would be twice as much, or £200. They'd continue to get the same £10 per year interest, but it would only work out at £2.50 every six months, or £5 a year, for each £100 they spent on the bond. You're getting twice the amount of interest compared with a new investor.

Now you have a choice. You can continue to enjoy your larger fixed-interest cheque every six months, getting more than you'd get as a new bond purchaser. Or you can cash in on your good luck. A new investor would pay £200 for your bond and get the fixed £10 per year. You can collect a £100 profit to reinvest elsewhere.

When interest rates rise

Suppose that rates rise from the 10 per cent at which you bought the bond to 20 per cent. No one would pay £100 for your bond because they could invest that money elsewhere to earn £20 per year. So because the interest rate has doubled, your bond is only worth half as much. You have the tough choice of taking a loss on the capital value or accepting that you'll get far less interest than a new investor.

I've simplified these examples to make the point. In real life, you must consider other factors including how much of the bond's life remains until redemption and the market's view of future interest-rate levels.

Interest rates often go up because the inflation index that measures rising prices increases. When you have high interest rates and high inflation, the paper value of your bond goes down. You're given a double hit:

- Interest levels rise so the capital value falls on the seesaw principle.
- The real value of each fixed payment and the final redemption amount also drops in purchasing terms because each currency unit (such as the pound, dollar or euro) buys less at the shops.

The credit rating conundrum

If only life for bond purchasers was as simple as second-guessing where interest rates and prices are due to go over the life of the bond. But, alas, life for bond purchasers isn't that simple. And that's why armies of highly paid analysts look over each bond with superpower spreadsheets.

Besides interest rates in the economy, a big factor for bond investors is whether the bond issuer will pay out the money on time or even at all. Bonds are issued by all sorts of organisations from the US Treasury to biotech or dotcom companies with a 1 in 20 chance of making it.

A bond is only as good as its issuer. There are no guarantees you can call on. In the past, bonds issued by big nations such as Germany, Russia and Argentina all failed. They became worth as much as wallpaper, except for a few attractive-looking certificates sold to collectors who framed and displayed them. (I have a Russian bond certificate from 1916, which I bought for £1. The frame cost a lot more.) More recently, the 2010 financial crisis in Europe started when international investors feared that Greece could not repay its bonds.

Alphabet soup: Looking at credit rating codes

You can get some help with working out which bonds have a higher credit rating. Agencies such as Standard & Poor's, Moody's and Fitch look at each bond issuer and the terms being offered, and then the agencies come up with a risk rating code.

The code isn't difficult to decipher. You just follow the alphabet. The highest level is AAA (or triple-A), followed by AA, A, BAA, BA, BBB, BB, B, with plenty more points all the way down to D. Plus and minus signs are used as well, showing whether a bond's been upgraded recently and is now less risky or whether it's been downgraded into a higher-peril situation. Each rating agency has its own little quirks, but the higher the letter in the alphabet and the more letters used, the lower the risk is.

Triple-A means a minimal risk. The US and UK governments and the biggest and best-financed companies pick up AAA. All the A grades are good, and some of the Bs are acceptable as well. Lots of bond investors draw the line at BBB, which, they say, is the lowest level of investment-grade bonds.

All the rest of them, many bond investors say, are undependable rubbish. With C grades, you run a reasonable risk of problems, and with D grades or ungraded bonds, you're gambling. You may miss a payment or two, or you may never see your money back on the redemption date. But note that bond experts don't call these bonds rubbish. Instead, they call them junk bonds (or, more politely, *high-yield* bonds).

Can you trust these ratings? They're as fallible as anything else in investment that tries to look forward. And the ratings agencies picked up some really bad publicity during the 2008 bank crisis when all too many of the complex instruments that came with high ratings turned out to be rubbish. But they're all anyone can hold on to – and their much talked about failures were in bonds so complex that each would need a whole volume of *Investing For Dummies* to explain. As long as you stick to plain vanilla bonds (and that's as far as this book goes) then the ratings agencies should be fine.

The higher the rating, the lower the interest rate. Investors want something extra to make up for the dangers of a poor credit rating but are willing to give up interest for the security of a top rating, such as triple-A or AAB. The rating looks at how long the bond has to pay out. A government or company may be good for a year or two, but will it still be paying out in 20 or 30 years' time? Agencies regularly revise risk ratings. What starts out at AAA can fall to junk levels and rubbish can rehabilitate itself and move up the scale.

Junk bonds: Where there's muck, there's brass (maybe!)

Why invest in junk bonds when the rating agencies say they're below investment grade? The obvious answer is the risk/reward equation. Junk-bond investors hope to spot bonds that are due for an upward re-rating that should push prices up.

Issuers of junk bonds pay higher interest rates to make up for the risk. And you can often buy the bonds at far below their face value. You pay, say, £30 for a £100 face-value bond from a company that may or may not live long enough to repay investors as it should. If the company survives, you've made £70 plus bigger interest payments all the way along the line. If it fails completely, you've lost your £30, but if you've had a few years of above-average payments along the way, then your loss doesn't look so bad. It might even work out that you've received your £30 back and more.

One junk bond may be a recipe for disaster. But put together a diversified collection in your portfolio, and there's a good chance that some winners will more than make up for the losers.

How low can you go?

At the top end of the quality scale, credit ratings are only for the ultra nervous. The gap between AAA and AA or A isn't really that crucial for most bond buyers. But anything below BBB is speculative. Investors have to pay more attention to junk-bond ratings as the risk of loss is real. So how low can you go?

✔ BB is probably still fine, but there are long-term fears over the issuing company or government. The company is more likely to be a bit late with the cash rather than not pay out at all.

✔ B should be okay as well, but if the economy or the business turns down, you may face problems. There are no guarantees, but you should get your payments. You can expect to get around 3 per cent per year extra on these bonds compared with AAA.

✔ CCC, CC, C is for caution. There's a current problem in the business or country issuing these bonds. An improvement on what you see now needs to occur before you can rest easier. You can expect around 4 to 7 per cent extra per year on these bonds.

✔ DDD, DD, D is for distress, disaster and default. Default is the bond dealer's shorthand for anything going wrong. The bond issuer is already in severe trouble, has missed out on payments and may be heading towards an early death. D-style bonds are only worthwhile buying if you're prepared to take a big gamble. You should aim for at least 10 to 15 per cent per year more here to make up for the ultra-risky rating.

Credit ratings apply to bonds from countries as well as companies. Countries can go bust or have problems repaying interest or debts. But some countries, such as former parts of the Soviet Union or nations in Africa, are young and don't have much of a credit record, so they get low marks. Always remember, bond buyers are naturally cautious. If they weren't, they'd be buying something racier.

The redemption calculation

Assuming that you're happy with the credit rating and the interest rate, you need to look at the redemption date of the bond. That's the day on which you'll receive, say, £100 for each £100 nominal on your bond certificate. It doesn't matter what you paid; you get £100.

The redemption date may be anywhere from days to decades away. Bonds fit into three main categories according to their final date:

- ✔ **Shorts or short-dated:** Anything up to 5 years.
- ✔ **Mediums:** From 5 to 15 years.
- ✔ **Longs:** From 15 years upward.

With the passage of time, a Long becomes a Medium and then a Short. The US is different (natch!). Over in New York, a long bond is called a long bond from day one all the way to the date it's finally repaid.

The date matters because the longer away it is, the greater the risk of either a default (the issuer missing a payment or not being able to repay) or an interest or credit rating change. Not much will happen over the next 30 days, so a very short-dated bond is unlikely to change much in price. The next 30 years, however, is a different matter. Bonds with a very long date can be very volatile, although that's only by bond standards! Shares can and do move up or down 10 per cent, 20 per cent or more in a day. Bond moves are small by comparison, but bond investors, more used to fractions of a percentage point, don't think so.

Longer-dated bonds should pay more interest to reflect the greater risks. This arrangement is called the *yield curve*, and the pay rate should go higher the further a bond has to run. Investors often look at why they're buying bonds and choose a life to fit. Someone with a 12-year-old child looking to fund educational fees may opt for a 10-year bond because it should coincide with a hoped-for university graduation and the need for funding in the big, bad world.

I want to briefly share one more thing related to this whole redemption calculation business. Bonds have two interest rates:

- ✔ **The running yield:** This is the amount you receive on your bond divided into the price you paid. So someone paying £90 for a £100 nominal value bond and earning £9 a year in interest would get a 10 per cent running yield.

✔ **The yield to redemption:** This one takes the running yield and then adjusts it for the gain or loss you make on final repayment. If you buy at over £100, your yield to redemption will be lower than your running yield; and if you buy at under £100, the redemption yield will be higher (assuming the bond will not go into default). A complicated formula exists for working out the yield to redemption, but most mortals just believe the figures they see in newspaper and online bond listings.

Knowing Which Way to Buy Your Bonds

Two main routes are available for buying bonds:

✔ **Purchase individual bonds through a stockbroker.** You'll pay the normal commission. Alternatively, if you're buying UK government bonds, special low-cost facilities are available through the Bank of England brokerage service, which is designed for small investors. The Bank of England website (www.bankofengland.co.uk) has details, or you can call 01452 398080. If you buy gilts at a debt-management-office auction when a government stock is first announced, you must apply for at least £1,000 (nominal).

✔ **Purchase bonds through a fund.** Hundreds of unit trusts specialise in bonds. They range from gilt funds, where the yield is low, to speculative junk bonds and bust-country bond funds. You buy these through independent financial advisers – don't go directly to fund companies because you'll end up paying more.

Chapter 10

Building an Information Bank

. . . .

In This Chapter

▶ Using your eyes and ears for information

▶ Searching the Internet

▶ Analysing tipsheets

▶ Examining media coverage

. . . .

*T*he Rothschilds' financial fortune and banking empire was founded, so it is said, on the family receiving news before all others of the defeat of Napoleon at Waterloo by the Duke of Wellington. The Rothschilds had organised a series of messengers and carrier pigeons so that they'd know the outcome first. The stock markets of the time believed the French would win and priced investments accordingly. But because the Rothschilds knew the real result first – that the opposite outcome had occurred – they were able to take big financial bets against the markets and make the early 19th century equivalent of billions.

Now, as then, investment markets revolve around information. If your information is quicker, more accurate and better understood than that of others, you'll prosper. So this chapter explains how to build your own personal information bank. The Internet, the media and ever-increasing disclosure rules for stock-market-quoted companies can give you more facts, figures and opinions than you'll ever want or be able to use. On top of that, companies produce annual reports and other documentation that grow weightier with each passing year.

Before you build your information bank, you must decide what you want from it. You can't file away everything available on financial markets, so limit yourself to looking at the shares and bonds you already hold, or at an area of the market that interests you, such as government stocks (the UK version of government stock is also known as a *gilt*, the US version a *treasury* and the German bond is called a *bund*), emerging markets or construction company shares. And after you build your information bank, you have to make up your mind what to do with the info. Know that if you're still confused, it's okay to keep your money in the bank. Know, too, that there's no such thing as an unrepeatable offer. You don't have to 'buy now while stocks last' because another deal is *always* coming along.

Taking a Look Around You

To build an information bank, your first move requires neither a computer nor a filing cabinet. It requires merely your eyes and ears.

You're surrounded by the products and services of stock-market-quoted companies. The high street is full of them. So too are your food cupboards, wardrobes and home leisure areas. The fortunes or otherwise of these firms are ultimately based on the purchasing decisions made by millions of consumers. And that includes you. Acting on gut feeling can be a valid start to a share buying or selling decision.

All the boasting and blustering of a firm's top management are meaningless if the employees nearest to the consumers fail to deliver good service or if the consumers themselves aren't interested or prefer a rival.

Here are some potential investing areas to look at:

✓ **Fashion retailing:** If you and your friends stop going to a store or start buying less, others are probably in a similar position are also shunning these outlets. Or, you may start buying at a store that you previously thought had poor design or bad value. For real examples, look at the ups and downs of high-street fashion staples such as Next and Marks & Spencer. They've both had periods in the doldrums and times when their goods were cutting edge. Companies can continue to churn out good profit figures for some time after customers have deserted them and may fail to reflect an increase for a year or two after consumers vote with their feet in favour.

✔ **Publishers:** Look at the Harry Potter phenomenon. Whether you like the books or not, millions of readers do. They turned publisher Bloomsbury from a small niche firm into a major player. But investors want to know where Bloomsbury goes now that the best-ever seller has reached the end of its series.

✔ **Food retailers:** The state of the car park and the length of the checkout queue at key times, such as Saturday mornings, can speak volumes about the success or otherwise of a superstore firm.

✔ **Holiday companies:** It's a bad sign if their nerve cracks and they start to offer deep discounts on school-holiday months such as August or if they're cutting prices many months ahead of departure dates.

✔ **Furniture, carpets and do-it-yourself superstores:** These largely depend on the number of people moving home who tend to buy new furniture and carpets and redecorate. A sluggish housing market is bad news here.

✔ **Natural resources shares:** These include mining and oil companies, whose shares tend to go up really fast when economies are booming and just as quickly down when trade halts or goes into reverse. Why? Because demand shoots up in good times and collapses in bad periods. These stocks are often seen as a substitute for direct investing in commodities such as copper or oil or coal.

✔ **January sales:** Whether they're selling cars or clothing, watch out for companies that have too many sales. Winter sales and summer sales should be enough. When the company gets to pre-Christmas, half-term, spring and autumn sales, start to worry. These firms aren't efficient.

Going Online

I used to have a chunky bookshelf lined with volumes on how to invest online. They were all very worthy and offered useful information, stressing how the Internet has revolutionised share buying and selling for the individual. Then I bundled the lot and sent them to the charity shop, simply because most of the stuff these books told me was out of date before I'd even read it. Sites they told me to visit that were free had erected paywalls (and vice versa). Sites had changed out of all recognition or had ceased to exist. So although in this section I mention a few of the sites I find particularly useful, countless sites offering investment advice exist and it's far better to find your own than rely on a list in a book.

In any case, I found most of the books failed to make these vital points:

- ✔ A huge amount of duplication is on the Internet, so concentrate your searches to a few sites that you know how to navigate and where you trust the content.

- ✔ Information on the Internet isn't guaranteed to be accurate or even have a passing resemblance to the truth. Before you accept anything, ask yourself what your reaction would be if you saw this in a hard copy. Would you trust it?

Chat rooms or so-called investment communities are a waste of time. They consist of clueless people posting messages to those looking for clues or, more dangerously, of chat from people with a position in the shares looking to give their investments a boost by persuading others to join them. Some of this information is downright misinformation – and often the very opposite of the truth. Ask yourself why a total stranger hiding behind a pseudonym should be so anxious to help you by sharing thoughts. Remember the old stock-market saying: 'Where there's a tip, there's a tap.' That means that people only give you information (the tip) if they see an advantage for them in your acting on their information (the tap).

- ✔ The Internet doesn't change the fundamentals of investment. It just speeds up the flow of information and increases the amount by a massive margin.

- ✔ Using the speed of the Internet to make buy or sell decisions can deprive you of those vital few seconds when you pinch yourself and double-check that you're doing the right thing.

- ✔ Thousands (literally) of financial scam sites exist, and they're devoted to parting you from your money.

Those are the warnings. But the Internet has great value in building up your personal investment information bank as well, especially if you use it counter-intuitively – in a way that most other investors don't think about doing because they're too busy confusing themselves in the noise and rubbish of investment communities. This section helps you use the power of the Internet to build your information bank.

Websites come and go. Their names change. Their services alter. Their policy on what's free and what you have to pay for also varies over time. And much of the info on the Internet that's useful to investors is repeated over and over again on various different sites. So use search engines on a regular basis – that way, you won't be stuck with a few sites and you can get a fresh view on the investment world.

Exploring the company's website

The dotcommers' vision of a shop-free world, where all products and services are traded online, has remained a pipe dream. But although most people still stick to traditional ways of buying, the Internet has a big influence on their decisions.

Exploring companies' websites can give you great insight into the companies themselves. To build your information bank, you need to assess the actual site, read the company's online report and read between the proverbial lines.

Assess the site itself

Your eyes and ears should play a big role in your information-bank building, so when you're exploring a company online, take a look at how well designed the website is. Start off with the product or consumer area. Act as though you want the product or service. If the site is easy to navigate, then it's likely to attract extra business. A bad site will send potential customers to the competition.

Assuming that the assessment passes your quality-control barriers, head off to the corporate section of the firm's site. This is often kept separate from the consumer side of things. If you enter 'ABC plc' into a search engine, you'll usually end up with the consumer site. But if you enter 'ABC plc corporate' you should find yourself where you want to be. On the corporate site, you should find a large amount of information about your target company, including press releases (usually doctored so that the press office phone number is left blank – to stop non-journalists from contacting the company), company statements, recent stock-exchange filings, and annual and interim reports. You should also find information on what the company does, its directors and senior managers, and how to contact the firm for more information. Usually included is an investor-relations section. (Investor relations is as much interested in would-be share buyers as in those already on the register.) While reading through all the information, again assess whether the company has made its info easy to access, navigate and understand.

Read the company's online report

Companies are legally obliged to produce an annual report and accounts, which they must send to shareholders (even if it's only an abbreviated version). These reports form an essential part of any information bank. Although firms aren't obliged to make these reports available on the Internet, view with scepticism any company that doesn't. The reason the company doesn't make its report available online may be that the company doesn't want you to see the report or to be aware that the company is late filing it.

Most online company reports are presented in pdf format, so you need Adobe Acrobat Reader software to read them. The software is easily available at no cost from many sites. It's best to update frequently to the latest version. When I got to Adobe 9.3, a friend was still using version 3.4. And she couldn't understand why so many pdfs were failing to open!

Read between the lines

Understanding the nuances of a company website is akin to understanding a bank reference or a school report. It's what's missing that counts!

Don't expect web material from a company to mention the negatives. Where these bad points have to be revealed publicly, the firm may well try to place them in a report in such a way that only the most wide-eyed reader will find them. In any case, no quoted company is yet obliged to keep a website. You can sometimes find negative opinions or information about a company by entering 'I hate ABC plc' or 'ABC plc sucks!' into a search engine.

So look out for:

- ✔ One person listed as both the chief executive and the chair of the company. This set-up runs contrary to present-day standards for company governance.

- ✔ Too many mentions of the company boss. Egomaniacs usually fail. Even worse are pictures of the company boss and his helicopter.

- ✔ Inadequate explanations of past problems. Firms will put as good a gloss as they can on negative news, so if you see or suspect anything untoward, search outside the company site.

- ✔ Glossing over director-level resignations. Again, check other sources.

- ✔ Promises of future growth without sufficiently good explanations as to how it will be achieved. Anyone can be optimistic. Coming up with concrete reasons is harder.

Your information bank will contain both positive and negative points on companies. No firm is faultless – it's always a question of balancing the good against the bad and then comparing with other companies that have a similar profile.

Exploring other sites for more info on the company

After you fully explore the company site, go back to your favourite search engine. Now you're looking for sites such as Adfvn, Bloomberg, Citywire or Yahoo. These sites offer a brief company history, up to five years of past results, charts of past share-price performance, names of company officers, directors' share dealings, comparisons with rival companies and present share-price information. You should be able to look at past performance over a number of timeframes with reference to the market as a whole. You can usually access information on these sites without paying, although you might have to pay for higher-level and more specialised information.

Most sites give share prices delayed by 15 minutes unless you pay for a premium service that gives real-time numbers. Paying for real-time prices is probably only worthwhile if you're a short-term trader rather than a longer-term investor.

Many share prices don't change much from day to day, and frequent movers often do so only within narrow limits.

Examining Tipsheets

Tipsheets and specialist share magazines, such as *Investors Tipsheets,* are small publications devoted to telling you exactly what to buy and sell. They tend to concentrate on small companies where a few purchases or sales can move the share price substantially. Some charge up to £1,000 a year for a few pages, or an email alert or two each month.

Literally dozens of tipsheets are on offer. They're regulated by the Financial Services Authority (or should be! Never take any notice of any that's outside the City watchdog's control). Tipsheet writers are supposed to reveal any holdings they have in shares they recommend, although this usually goes no further than a vague statement. And tipsheets are meant to indicate when shares are difficult to buy and sell. This is because tipsters tend to push shares in illiquid situations where the gap between what buyers pay and what sellers get (this is called the *spread*) can be enormous.

Pushing shares like this can enable tipsters to mark up great successes! For instance, if they push a share at 4p and it goes up to 5p, they can claim a 25 per cent gain. That sounds brilliant. But now look at the reality. The share that appears at 4p costs 4.5p to buy. And when the share goes up to 5p, sellers only get 4.5p. On this example, the 25 per cent gain has disappeared altogether! And that's before the cost of buying and selling. In some cases, it could be even worse with a share that appears to rise but actually costs the investor.

Here are a few additional titbits about tipsheets:

- ✔ Most tipsheets have low-cost introductory offers. You sign up for a direct debit for three to six months at a bargain rate, which, unless you cancel it, automatically moves to the far more expensive rate after that.

- ✔ Some go for a scatter-gun approach and tip a large number of shares in each issue, hoping that one or two are bound to be winners. Others are more careful.

✔ There's no evidence that any tipsheet is consistently good. But if you like the idea, try a few to find one that suits your risk/reward profile and the sort of share you like to invest in. One or two tipsheets specialise in sectors such as technology or investment trusts.

✔ Tipsheets advertise their successes and ignore their failures. They aren't obliged to reveal the date when the tip was made in any advert or when the sheet suggested selling, so know that the successes may be several years old when market conditions were quite different.

Looking at News Coverage

All UK-quoted companies have to report at least twice yearly (some report quarterly) to shareholders and issue statements on occasions such the issuing of new shares, during takeovers and significant director-level changes. This information is revealed to the stock market via the Regulatory News Service (RNS), which gives equal prominence to an announcement from a company worth £10 billion or more and to one worth £10 million or less. Big stockbroking firms and investing institutions subscribe. You can do so too, but it costs a fortune and delivers little in return for the cost.

Most people rely on newspapers as a primary source of information and for comment on the stock market and other investment issues. But even the most comprehensive newspapers only cover a small proportion of a day's RNS output. So it's vital to know how City pages work, the decisions editors make and why some companies receive so much more coverage than others.

Rule 1 is that City pages aren't just written for investors. They have to attract at least some other readers to justify their expense. Companies with a high-street presence, such as retailers and banks, get more coverage than manufacturing concerns or mining companies, no matter how important these companies might be, because non-investor readers like to know how famous names are doing.

Rule 2 is that reporters can't be everywhere at once. They concentrate on companies they consider sexy. They may even take that word literally. For example, reporters write about some companies because they're in the fashion world – a cue for a picture of a scantily clad model. A firm making millions of pounds by making billions of nuts and bolts doesn't make a pretty picture. Reporters also concentrate on controversial companies, including those whose directors are deemed to be greedy fat cats or where big losses are occurring. All this coverage is at the expense of other firms that simply grow a little each year. There's generally little coverage of small companies unless they're especially newsworthy, perhaps because of a celebrity involvement.

Rule 3 is that public relations agencies play a major and growing role. Most quoted companies hire PR firms whose job it is to ensure that good news gets into newspapers and bad news is hidden away or, preferably, ignored or even better gets turned into good news. These firms try to influence the comment columns most City pages run. Many journalists have close relationships with public relations advisers.

Rule 4 is that very few journalists now dig deep enough to expose powerful people and companies doing things they shouldn't be. One reason for this is that investigations cost substantially in time and money – most media organisations now have little time and practically no money – so probes don't get past first base. And the second reason is the increasing power of lawyers to silence criticism. Articles on the taxation methods of retailers and the pollution caused by oil firms are among those that have faced severe (and highly costly) legal action. Owing to legal differences, US newspaper and online journalists have greater freedom.

Most newspapers have online archives so you can look at how a company was reported in the past.

Can you trust what you read?

This chapter mentions several points to be wary of when looking at information that's offered to you on a plate. Remember that you're being told something by a perfect stranger that could make you poorer or richer. Always ask why you're being told this, and what's in it for the person telling you. More generally, always remember that very little is black and white in investment. A lot of what you'll be told is opinion, and whether you can trust it may depend on the track record of the person giving you this material.

Part III
Collective Investments

'Actually my business card's in there if you're
interested in investing your money . . .'

In this part . . .

*W*ith packaged investments, professional fund managers look after your money in return for a fee. Often, a bewildering variety of funds is available for you to choose from. And the management companies behind them spend a fortune trying to convince you that theirs is top dog.

The best fund managers are experts, but with the worst, you'd be much better off keeping your money under the bed! So don't expect gift wrapping or one of those reassuring guarantees. Never forget the professionals have their own agenda. This part tells you to take nothing at face value and always look at everything with a big pinch of salt.

Chapter 11

Getting into Unit Trusts

· ·

In This Chapter

▶ Understanding how to own lots of shares for little cash

▶ Learning about unit-trust charges

▶ Sorting out active from passive unit-trust fund managers

▶ Looking at ethical unit trusts

· ·

*U*nit and investment trusts are the most important route for UK investors to buy a ready-made portfolio of shares or bonds backed by professional management. Together they're known as *collective investment.*

So what do unit and investment trusts give you that you can't do yourself? The best answer is they offer a diversified selection of investments so you spread your risk. The only way that you could replicate this is if you were so rich that you could invest meaningful amounts (and I'm talking £100,000 minimum here) into at least 30 to 40 shares. That adds up to about £3 to 4 million.

On top of that, you get someone – at a cost – to look after your investments for you. Effectively, you choose the area of investment – the UK, Japan or Russia, for instance – and someone to manage your money while the fund does all the legwork. And it can literally be legwork: fund managers often visit the companies they invest in, or might invest in, to check up on progress.

Both unit and investment trusts offer these ready-made managed portfolios. And although differences between the two exist – this chapter will point them out – the similarities are more significant. Unless you really want to do it all yourself and have the £4 million stuffed under your mattress, then you'll probably want to stick with trusts for the major part of your investment strategy.

The great thing about both forms of trust is that you can get started for as little as £50 (occasionally even £25) if you sign up for a monthly investment scheme, or £250 to £500 as a lump sum. Doing so gives you access to a professionally managed fund that diversifies your money into anything from some 30 shares to more than 200 holdings. You get a huge number of shares for not much money.

Don't get too impressed by funds with the longest list of holdings. There's no correlation between a large number of holdings and management success. In fact, some people think that having too many shares just spreads research and other fund-manager functions a bit too thinly.

This chapter tells you what unit and investment trusts are and how they work, to help you decide whether investing in them is right for you, and points you towards sectors that meet your needs.

Understanding What Unit Trusts Are

Unit trusts are so called because you hold a number of units in a fund that's legally set up as a trust. Simple. But don't get too hung up on the word *trust* because you can't always trust them to come up with the investment goods.

People sometimes refer to unit trusts with other names. *Mutual funds* is the title preferred in the United States, and it's becoming more common in the UK. *Open-ended funds* (because the number of units has no limit) is also a US term that's moving across the Atlantic. And in the UK, more and more funds are, strictly speaking, defined as *open-ended investment companies (OEICs)*. But almost everyone still calls them unit trusts.

If you're really interested in all the fine print of a trust, you can get a copy of the trust deed. But don't bother (unless you're a committed fan of legalese). It won't help you in your quest for investment gains.

Leaving aside the legal stuff, unit trusts are a simple concept. A fund-management firm advertises a trust, and lots of investors send in money either directly or through brokers. After the firm subtracts around 5 per cent for set-up costs and commission to brokers, it invests the rest in whatever assets the managers are promoting. The assets can be anything from global equities to UK gilts to commercial property.

For example, suppose that a person invests £1,000 when the units are priced at £1 each. The investor now has 1,000 units, the value of which goes up and down in direct proportion to the underlying fund. The size of the fund obviously depends on the success or otherwise of the managers in picking the right investments. But it also depends on whether money from the other investors is flowing in or out because they're buying or selling. No matter what happens to the size of the fund, however, you always have your 1,000 units, which can change in price. Unlike direct investment in shares, however, where your holding remains a fixed (if small) percentage of the company's capital, your units will vary as a proportion of the entire trust. Firms can create and destroy units as demand rises and falls.

Knowing How Much Unit Trusts Cost

You can't expect collective investment for nothing. Unit trusts have up to three charges – an initial charge, an annual charge and an exit charge (which is now so rare that it's best ignored – it won't happen any more).

Charges can be complicated, but here's a simple word of advice. The worst deal you'll get is to buy your unit trust (or OEIC) directly from the fund-management company. It's throwing money down the drain. Buying unit trusts direct is never better than the discount or investment supermarket routes. An _investment_ or _fund supermarket_ is an online facility where you can select funds to invest in yourself. However, you're legally the client of a financial adviser or stockbroker. Most advisers offer a choice of the two main supermarkets: Cofunds and FundsNetwork. Other advisers offer just one. There's really not a lot to choose between them.

The initial charge

The upfront, or initial, charge is levied when you buy the fund.
The charge can be either built in via the bid–offer spread
or added on as a brokerage charge when you buy an OEIC.
With most funds, you're charged about 5 per cent no matter
whether you buy through a broker or directly from the fund
company. But some exceptions to the 5 per cent level exist:

- ✔ Funds aimed at charity treasurers and professionals
  (such as brokers) who can invest large sums have no or
  low charges.

- ✔ Funds investing in UK government stocks and some other
  bonds generally undershoot the 5 per cent line, with
  some charging 1 per cent or even 0 per cent.

Many brokers rebate some or all of the 3 per cent commission
they receive from the upfront charge on most funds. They're
not working for nothing, however. Funds are now structured
to pay *trail commission*, which means the seller receives 0.5
per cent of the value of your fund every year as long as you
hold it. Brokers are supposed to give something back in terms
of service and advice. Many (probably most) don't. But some
issue helpful material every three months.

The annual charge

All unit trusts have a yearly charge. It can vary from 0.295 per
cent or 0.3 per cent for the best-value UK tracker funds to 1.75
per cent for some esoteric trusts. Most trust rules allow for
higher charges, provided that you're given some notice. Over
the years, annual charges have tended to rise. Managers have
to pay the trail commission out of something. And there's VAT
on top of that.

Hidden charges

With most funds, the annual charge is taken from the dividends received. So if the underlying fund earns 4 per cent and
your charge is 1 per cent, you end up with 3 per cent. (This is
a simplified example ignoring VAT.) Funds are generally managed to ensure that there's some income to meet the costs.

But with a minority of funds, mostly investing in bonds and other high-income assets, you're given all the income. This isn't generosity but sleight of hand. Instead of the fund taking the charge from the income, it's shaved away from your capital. The result? Fund-management companies can proudly proclaim a higher return on your cash than those going the conventional route of hitting your income. Looks good in adverts! Clever, huh!

Check on charges. Some funds are better value. No relationship whatsoever exists between high annual charges and better-than-average performance.

Identifying Unit-Trust Sectors

The unit-trust world is divided into sectors that cover the broad range of all that's on offer, from the safe to the scary. Each main sector is then subdivided so, for example, capital growth would include Japan and Europe as separate lists. You can't really compare Japan's shares with those of Europe (think of apples and oranges), but both these sectors might appeal to investors looking for growth and higher risk from overseas equities rather than income and lower risk from government bonds, for example.

The low-risk sectors

In this section, I look at unit-trust sectors that appeal to the safety-first investor. Here are the funds principally targeting capital protection:

- ✔ **Money market:** These invest at least 95 per cent of their assets in money-market instruments (cash and near cash, such as bank deposits, certificates of deposit, very short-term fixed-interest securities or floating-rate notes). But never forget that these assets can go down – near cash isn't really cash! So this isn't the home for money you need in the near term – it should be fine for a year or so, though.

- ✔ **Protected:** Funds, other than money-market funds, that principally aim to provide a return of a set amount of capital to the investor (either explicitly protected or via an investment strategy highly likely to achieve this objective) plus the potential for some investment return. Remember that protected isn't the same as guaranteed. And there's no point going for one of these funds if you really believe your chosen investment will soar – you pay for the protection in lots of ways including ceilings, which mean your gains are limited to a set figure.

Income funds

Moving up the risk/reward ladder, the next sector consists of unit trusts that aim to produce a mix of dividend income and some limited capital growth as well. These trusts can be useful if you need a regular boost to your earnings or pension. Here are the funds principally targeting income (by asset category):

- ✔ **UK gilts:** These invest at least 95 per cent of their assets in sterling-denominated (or hedged back to sterling), triple-A-rated, government-backed securities, with at least 80 per cent invested in UK government securities (gilts).

- ✔ **UK index-linked gilts:** These invest at least 95 per cent of their assets in sterling-denominated triple-A-rated government-backed index-linked securities, with at least 80 per cent invested in UK index-linked gilts. They should protect your savings against rising prices with a little bit over. Super-safe.

- ✔ **Sterling corporate bond:** These invest at least 80 per cent of their assets in sterling-denominated (or hedged back to sterling), triple-B-minus or above corporate-bond securities (as measured by Standard & Poor's or an equivalent external rating agency). This excludes con-vertibles, preference shares and permanent interestbear-ing shares (PIBs). Some risk.

- ✔ **Sterling strategic bond:** These invest at least 80 per cent of their assets in sterling-denominated fixed-interest securities such as convertibles, preference shares and permanent interest-bearing shares (PIBs). There's some risk but the chance of rewards.

- ✔ **Sterling high yield:** These invest at least 80 per cent of their assets in sterling-denominated bonds with at least 50 per cent of their assets in below BBB-minus fixed-interest securities including convertibles, preference shares and permanent interest-bearing shares (PIBs). High yield is the polite term for junk bonds.

✔ **Global bonds:** These invest at least 80 per cent of their assets in fixed-interest securities in any country of the world except the UK.

✔ **UK equity and bond income:** These invest at least 80 per cent of their assets in the UK, between 20 per cent and 80 per cent in UK fixed-interest securities and between 20 per cent and 80 per cent in UK equities. These funds aim to have a yield in excess of 120 per cent of the FTSE All Share Index. Here you should get some growth with six-monthly payments, which you can spend or reinvest into the trust.

Equity sectors

Equity funds are riskier than those I've mentioned so far but also offer the potential of greater long-term reward. These two sectors aim to mix 'n' match growth prospects with growing dividends. Some investors use a facility to plough back their dividends into new units until the day when they need the income.

✔ **UK equity income:** These invest at least 80 per cent in UK equities and aim to achieve a historic yield on the distributable income in excess of 110 per cent of the FTSE All Share yield at the fund's year end.

✔ **UK equity income and growth:** These invest at least 80 per cent of their assets in UK equities; aim to have a historic yield on the distributable income in excess of 90 per cent of the yield of the FTSE All Share Index at the fund's year end; and aim to produce a combination of both income and growth.

Funds targeting growth

These sectors aim for outright growth with little or no consideration for dividends or any other form of regular income. In some cases, the dividends are so low that they don't even pay for the annual fund-management charges.

✔ **UK all companies:** These invest at least 80 per cent of their assets in UK equities, which have a primary objective of achieving capital growth. Tracker funds are usually in this sector. This is the biggest sector with over 400 funds.

✔ **UK smaller companies:** These invest at least 80 per cent of their assets in UK equities of companies that form the bottom 10 per cent by market capitalisation. Here you're taking a chance on the market's Tiddlers – they often go up before larger companies but can crash farther and faster than the big firms.

Overseas equities

Going overseas increases risks still further because investors have to concern themselves with currencies and exchange rates as well. Here's a listing of the main equity sectors from outside the UK.

✔ **Japan:** These invest at least 80 per cent of their assets in Japanese equities.

✔ **Japanese smaller companies:** These invest at least 80 per cent of their assets in Japanese equities of companies that form the bottom 30 per cent by market capitalisation.

✔ **Asia Pacific including Japan:** These invest at least 80 per cent of their assets in Asia Pacific equities including a Japanese content. The Japanese content must make up less than 80 per cent of assets.

✔ **Asia Pacific excluding Japan:** These invest at least 80 per cent of their assets in Asia Pacific equities and exclude Japanese securities.

✔ **North America:** These invest at least 80 per cent of their assets in North American equities. This is really Wall Street but can include Canadian companies.

✔ **North American smaller companies:** These invest at least 80 per cent of their assets in North American equities of companies that form the bottom 20 per cent by market capitalisation.

✔ **Europe including UK:** These invest at least 80 per cent of their assets in European equities. They may include UK equities, but these mustn't exceed 80 per cent of the fund's assets. This sector's small – it's really better to go

for Europe and the UK separately rather than invest in a
fund that's neither one nor the other.

- ✔ **Europe excluding UK:** These invest at least 80 per cent
  of their assets in European equities and exclude UK
  securities.

- ✔ **European smaller companies:** These invest at least 80
  per cent of their assets in European equities of companies that form the bottom 20 per cent by market capitalisation in the European market. You could get some UK
  shares in these funds.

- ✔ **Global growth:** These invest at least 80 per cent of their
  assets in equities and have the prime objective of achieving growth of capital. You buy this sector when you just
  want foreign investment. You need to look closely at
  each fund's fact sheet to see what you really get.

- ✔ **Global emerging markets:** These invest 80 per cent or
  more of their assets directly or indirectly in emerging
  markets as defined by the World Bank, without geograph-
  ical restriction. Effectively, most of the money goes into
  Brazil, Russia, India and China (probably via Hong Kong)
  but it could go into many countries, some of which you
  may never have heard of. Can be very risky.

Mixed-asset sectors

Investors who aren't sure where they want to place their
money can opt for someone else to make those big decisions
for them. With the mixed-asset sectors, the main choice concerns level of risk.

- ✔ **Cautious managed:** These invest in a range of assets with
  the maximum equity exposure restricted to 60 per cent
  of the fund and with at least 30 per cent invested in fixed
  interest and cash. The fund should do what it says on the
  tin and produce some gains, but gains that are generally
  of a moderate nature and not those that will collapse
  overnight should markets turn suddenly.

- ✔ **Balanced managed:** This is the next stage up the risk
  ladder from cautious managed. Here funds offer investment in a range of assets, with the maximum equity exposure restricted to 85 per cent of the fund. At least 10 per
  cent of the total fund must be held in non-UK equities.

✔ **Active managed:** This ratchets up the risk/reward ratio another few notches. These funds offer investment in a range of assets, with up to 100 per cent in equities with at least 10 per cent of the total fund in non-UK equities.

Specialist sectors

These narrow funds invest in one specialised area or use techniques that go beyond the usual buy-and-hope-it-goes-up method that most fund managers adopt.

✔ **Absolute return:** These are managed with the aim of delivering absolute (more than zero) returns in any market conditions. Typically, funds in this sector normally expect to deliver absolute (more than zero) returns on a 12-month basis. This sector, with techniques derived from hedge-fund managers, has become very popular with investors who can't decide whether markets are rising or falling. The returns won't be spectacular but neither – if the managers are competent – will you suffer from big falls. But no guarantees exist.

✔ **Property:** These predominantly invest in property. Many of these funds have small-print clauses that allow the managers to close the fund for a period (often six months) if too many investors want their money out. This is because it can take time to sell properties such as the office blocks or shopping centres in which these trusts typically invest.

In order to invest predominantly in property, funds should do either of the following:

- Invest at least 60 per cent of their assets directly in property.

- Invest at least 80 per cent of their assets in shares or bonds from property companies.

✔ **Specialist:** This is the heading given to funds that don't fit into a mainstream sector, such as South Korea, Switzerland, Germany, Thailand and Australia, along with single-industry funds covering mining, healthcare, biotechnology and financial services. This is a ragbag because there's no way you can compare a Swiss shares fund with a worldwide natural resources trust. All aim at growth and many are rated a 'scary risk'.

When several stocks cover the same area, they might sometimes qualify for their own sector. So healthcare, financial companies and mining shares have their own breakout listings. Mining funds can often be a good way of getting into a commodity boom as they invest in gold, copper, zinc and other raw materials.

✔ **Technology and telecommunications:** These invest at least 80 per cent of their assets in technology and telecommunications sectors as defined by major index providers. Some are survivors from the dotcom boom of 1999, when fund managers launched into what was then the latest craze. But their managers say an interest in backing technology will always exist, whether for communications or to help deal with global warming, so some funds now specialise in alternative energy sources. Risky to very risky.

Comparing Active Versus Passive Fund Managers

Active fund managers buy and sell shares and other assets hoping that they'll perform at least better than average and preferably hit the big time. Most funds are actively managed.

Passive fund managers don't care. The reason is that they're usually computers, not people, without too much in the way of sentimental feeling. They buy all the constituents of an index in the right proportions (or occasionally come up with sampling methods to ensure that a fund doesn't have to cope with hundreds of tiny company shares).

The result of passive fund management (this is another name for the tracker-fund concept, so called because no one has to do anything to select the shares because they're automatically chosen) is that what you get is what you see. If the fund tracks the Footsie (the FTSE 100 share index of the UK's biggest stock-market-quoted firms), then your fund will go up and down each day along with the index. You'll get an income calculated as the average yield on the basket of shares your fund follows, less the annual management charge. You'll also know what level of risk you're taking.

Most passive funds in the UK track either the Footsie or the wider All Share Index. But you can buy passive funds that follow markets in other countries; that buy into sectors worldwide, such as technology or pharmaceuticals; or that only invest in an index of ethically and environmentally approved companies. A growing area of passive investment is to buy the replication of an index through exchange-traded funds. Exchange-traded funds are traded via stockbrokers just as if they were real shares. They're big in America and getting bigger in the UK.

Active versus passive has always been the big fund-management debate. Both sides can come up with good (and sometimes bad) arguments:

- Active managers say that they can add value because they can sift out the wheat from the chaff.

- Passive managers say that they don't have to second-guess the future.

- Active managers say that they have a wider range of investments, including smaller companies with a great future.

- Passive managers say that most of these small-company bets fail. And even when they do well, they have little effect on the overall fund because holdings are minuscule.

- Active managers say that they offer strategies that vary with market conditions.

- Passive managers say that the market as a whole automatically adjusts to different conditions.

- Active managers say that passive funds end up with too many shares that have peaked. The trick is to look for shares that are growing fast enough to knock on an index's door.

- Passive managers say that a lot of active managers just buy big-index stocks but charge up to five times extra for the privilege – a practice called *closet indexing* in the investment trade. You can sometimes spot a closet indexer because all their big holdings (see the fact sheet that usually lists at least the ten most significant investments) are virtually the same as the biggest stocks in the index.

✔ Active managers say that passive funds often fail to track their chosen index properly. There's no real defence to that other than to claim the opposite!

✔ Passive managers say that they win on costs. They reckon that active managers have to do about 1.5 per cent better a year than the index – a tough call year on year. That's because passive-management costs in a unit trust are typically under 0.5 per cent annually.

✔ Active managers say that they can spread their investments more efficiently. They don't have to buy and sell whenever firms go in and out of an index. They can talk to companies and sometimes influence the stock market. But, they say, passive fund managers must buy stocks they have no control over and at whatever price the market dictates.

✔ Passive managers say that although they'll never top a table, they'll never be below halfway for long either. They say that active funds that beat them one year probably won't do so the next. Owing to costs and other factors, a good index fund should always end up around 38th to 42nd place in a group of 100 funds over a typical year. Performing this way consistently is better than rocket performance one year and rubbish performance the next – unless you're quick enough to spot the gains and then move to avoid the falls, but actually no one's really that clever.

Taking Ethics into Consideration

'Ethics? That's a county to the east of London!'

That's an old City joke and probably not one of the brightest. But all jokes have some element of truth, and this one says that the mainstream neither invests nor even cares about selecting investments with a green or ethical tinge.

But many private investors and members of a growing number of pension funds want to feel that their money is backing firms they approve of. The ethical investment market has gone from zero to about £50 billion over the past 25 or so years. Some £6 billion of this sum is in unit trusts representing 5 per cent or so of all equity investment in mutual funds. The UK has a long way to go to catch up with the US, however, where 12 per cent or more of equity funds are managed ethically.

Ethically investing in the right companies

Ethical investors want to avoid investing in companies involved in tobacco, armaments, hardwood logging, animal experimentation, nuclear power, gambling and pornography, or in organisations that support repressive regimes or that manufacture goods using sweatshops in less-developed countries. Equally, ethical investment (often called *socially responsible investment*, or *SRI*) is buying into firms involved in positives, including alternative renewable energy such as wind farms, and recycling and waste management. SRI also includes buying into firms at the forefront of good employment practice and those providing high-quality services or goods that clearly benefit the wider community.

Balancing act: The pros and cons of ethical investing

Some investors are passionate about SRI. They should skip this section. Others believe that a sin-stock portfolio of tobacco, armaments and pornography publishers works best. They should skip this section as well. You can read what you like into past performance statistics, depending on the period you select and the funds you look at, so it's really a matter of balancing the pros and cons of ethical investing:

- ✓ **Pro:** Stocks screened out come from dinosaur old-economy industries, such as mining, tobacco, chemicals and armaments, where growth is more limited and government controls are stricter.

- ✓ **Con:** Fund managers can't perform their job if they're limited by non-investment criteria imposed by non-investment people. And sometimes sectors such as tobacco or mining do very well – they were some of the better investments in the first decade of this century.

- ✓ **Pro:** SRI-approved stocks tend to be young, dynamic firms that benefit from the general move away from dirty industries towards a cleaner future.

- ✓ **Con:** SRI companies may be less profit-conscious because they're too concerned with their employees or the neighbourhood they work in. And too many go bust because they have a good idea but either can't carry it through or find the market for their goods isn't there or has moved on.

✔ **Pro:** Companies that show the management abilities to move to a more sustainable way of doing business are probably brighter and less stuck in the mud elsewhere.

✔ **Con:** SRI funds concentrate too much on volatile smaller companies.

Going with a Fund of Funds

Most unit-trust investors start off with a UK fund, often a tracker. Then they add to it with more UK-based trusts, and then they venture overseas. But as they build up their portfolio, they have to make decisions. They have to choose the best in each sector that they select and then monitor their holdings.

The do-it-yourself approach has two big failings. Massive costs are involved every time an investor switches from one fund to another. And there's capital gains tax on profits. The alternative is to hand over money to a fund of funds manager, who invests in other funds but in such a way that minimises switching costs and has no capital gains tax worries within the fund.

Do funds of funds beat a buy and hold strategy? The jury's out. But the fund managers must be specially gifted to overcome the drag of two sets of charges. You pay annual fees on the fund of funds and yearly charges on the underlying funds. If you pick a manager badly, you'll end up paying more for less investment performance.

So far, no one's come up with a fund of funds of funds!

Examining Monthly Investment Plans

Most funds have investment plans for regular savers, with some starting as low as £25 a month. These take your money from your bank account through a direct debit on a monthly basis and buy units in the plan (or shares in an investment trust) at whatever the price is on the day of purchase.

They're sometimes called *savings plans*, although, unlike bank or building society savings, you aren't guaranteed ever to get your money back. These are risky investments.

Although some have very low minimum amounts, the majority of plans insist on at least £50 a month, and a few aim as high as £250. Savings plans have no minimum savings periods, so you can stop when you like and either cash in or leave your money to grow (hopefully!).

Besides the ability to fund a scheme with small sums, you also benefit from not having to worry so much about timing. Your regular sum buys more units when prices are low and fewer when they're high, so you iron out the ups and downs of investment prices. Stopping or selling will need a positive decision, however, as you'll have to decide on what time's best for your needs.

Regular investment plans are very flexible because you can change your amount each month (as long as it stays above the minimum for your plan). You could, in theory, stay in for just one month. In practice, people invest affordable sums for many years. It's often money they don't really miss each month. But when they do cash in, they're often amazed at how well they've done.

Note that savings plans are rarely available through discount brokers or supermarkets. So you must expect to pay the full upfront and annual fees for your investment.

Finding Out More About Unit Trusts

If you'd like to find out more about unit trusts, a good place to start for general information is the Investment Managers Association (IMA), a trade body taking in most unit-trust management firms. The website is www.investmentuk.org; the phone number is 020 7831 0898. The IMA publishes a number of useful booklets.

In addition, every fund manager has a website, and most fund managers post their monthly thoughts about investments as well as details of how to invest. Many independent financial advisers (IFAs) simply repeat this material to clients as if it were their own.

Chapter 12

Looking at Fund Management

. . . .

In This Chapter

▶ Understanding the benefits of diversification

▶ Looking at the fund manager's role

▶ Delving into fund marketing techniques

▶ Scrutinising performance figures

▶ Questioning what fund managers say

. . . .

*Y*ou can identify a fund-management advert from a mile away. It features a huge graph with the line heading to the stratosphere. It may even include a rocket heading for outer space just in case you're too dim to understand the concept. (Some fund managers push the point home even further by naming themselves after planets or stars.) And the warnings, of course, are listed in tiny print.

Whatever the approach, fund promoters hope that you'll just send them your cheque as mindlessly as you'd buy a packet of crisps – perhaps less so.

Not if you're reading this book, you won't!

The history of investing is full of 'good ideas' that didn't work. At the turn of the century there was the tech fund bubble (cue pictures of scantily dressed women whose clothes were found on some online store at half the high-street price), and more recently, a fund that invested in Africa (cue beautiful wild animals) but forgot that buying and selling shares in Africa can be impossible.

Packaged, or *collective*, investments (the terms are interchangeable) – where a professional fund manager mingles your money with that of many others to run a portfolio of stocks and shares – have their place for most investors. In fact, some people don't want anything else but packaged schemes, such as unit and investment trusts. There's nothing wrong with that, provided you know why you're doing it and can deconstruct all the advertising and marketing tricks. That's where this chapter comes in. Read on.

Understanding How Fund-Management Companies Operate

The packaged-funds industry in the UK controls a few trillion pounds in unit trusts, investment trusts, pension funds and insurance funds. (Note that unit trusts are also known as *open-ended investment companies*, which is a bit of a mouthful, so the term is often shortened to OEICs. And, okay, technically, a unit trust and an OEIC have different legal structures, but show me anyone other than a specialist lawyer who cares.)

All packaged funds work in the same basic fashion. You hand over your money to a fund-management company, which can be a stand-alone company, a life-insurance firm or a bank. The fund-management company adds your money to that of many others so the managers it employs can try to maximise your investment in a cost-effective way. The result is a multimillion or even multibillion plus fund.

Because you and others have teamed up, you can now afford the professionals whose salaries would be prohibitive if you tried to hire them on your own – or a computer program if your fund just tracks an index by purchasing all of the companies that are its constituents (such as the hundred shares in the FTSE 100 Index) in their correct ratios (so your biggest holding is the largest company by stock-market size in the index).

Flesh-and-blood fund managers look at the same factors as any potential investor. But because they control millions or billions, they get preferential treatment from brokers and research houses – they get to hear things before you can and ought to have the expertise to make better decisions than you can. But they also have to go further in their work than individual shareholders because they must keep a number of juggling balls in the air if they want to keep their usually very well-paid jobs. And what's written on those juggling balls? The following words:

✔ **Performance:** The manager must beat the majority of direct rivals or come up with very plausible excuses. All investment managers know those soaring graphs sell funds.

✔ **Liabilities:** Many funds, especially those from insurance companies, have rules that insist they balance the desire to shine with a responsibility to produce a basic return for investors and policyholders. These regulations may prevent them from investing in some areas, acting either (you choose) like a brake on their creativity or a sensible limit on their gambling instinct.

✔ **Cost controls:** Some fund-management companies can spend money like it's going out of fashion. Most funds have constraints to prevent managers from dealing all day long, eroding the collective's value in stockbroker fees. But these controls can be vague.

✔ **Publicity:** Managers want an eye-catching performance to attract more money and hence push up the value of their personal employment contract. Yes, it's the soaring graph again!

Your deal is with the fund-management company, not individual fund managers, even when they're hailed as superstars. Managers may leave for a better job (if they're good) or get the sack (if they're bad), and even superstars have bad periods, retire or fall under buses. Over recent years, there's been a lively transfer market in good managers and a big cleanout of those who can be outplayed by a five-year-old picking shares with a pin. Fewer than half of all funds have had the same manager for five or more years.

Funds can also be shut down or amalgamated, as I know to my cost. Many years ago I put money into a Latin American fund. Latin America was in the doldrums but I reckoned long term that it would turn out fine. It did – except that, on the way, the manager of my fund decided the fund couldn't make enough money out of Latin America so they shut the investment down.

I got some money back eventually but not nearly as much as if I'd been able to back my hunch all the way.

Calculating their crust

Most fund-management companies earn their money by taking an annual percentage fee from your holding. This fee can range from 0.3 to 2 per cent or more of your money. They earn this percentage whether your fund is rising or falling. Obviously, the more it goes up, the more they get. They also receive a boost when new investors join, assuming that they outweigh those who want their money out.

Investors argue that it costs little more to manage a £200 million fund than a £20 million fund, so why does the management firm get ten times as much? It's a good point, and a small minority of fund-management companies, mostly in the investment-trust sector, offer lower fees as the amount grows – a feature called *economies of scale* and one worth looking out for.

A new way of looking at fund expenses and costs exists that does recognise economies of scale as well as the set annual fee. This new way is called the total expenses ratio, or TER, and takes in such items as custody fees, the money the fund spends on buying and selling securities, and various legal costs. The TER is a better way of looking at which fund offers the best value because a fund with a 1 per cent annual charge could have 2 per cent in other expenses, giving a 3 per cent TER, whereas a rival might have a 1.5 per cent annual charge but only 0.5 per cent in other costs, so it would have a 2 per cent TER. And with costs, 2 per cent of your money is better than 3 per cent. Look out for the TER in information about unit trusts.

Swapping collective funds can be very expensive. Some fund-management companies charge you up to 5.5 per cent as an upfront entry fee, so your investment must grow by that amount before you break even. Changing your mind twice a year over ten years would more than wipe out all your original money in costs unless your investment grows substantially. Funds are for the long term, so budget to stay with a collective for at least five years or learn to use one of the online fund supermarkets where switching costs are far lower. Moving in and out of profitable funds may land you with a capital gains tax bill – but it's far better to pay tax on your gains than nurse tax-free losses.

Examining the role of the marketing department

You won't see ABC plc advertising its own shares. Although the directors obviously want to see a healthy price, all sorts of rules prevent it from marketing its own equity. In any case, once the shares have been issued, ABC's got its money – day-to-day price fluctuations don't affect its balance sheet.

Collective investments are different. Here, the promoters spend a fortune on advertising their wares. All this is regulated by a rule book the size of a telephone directory, but don't be fooled. You're out there on your own.

So, don't be afraid to ask questions and query what you're told. It's your money after all, not theirs.

You should know about marketing tricks before you start. Here are some:

✔ Dividing all publicity between the big print designed to get effect and the small print, which absolves the fund-management company of any responsibility if things go wrong.

✔ Launching a flavour of the month. Fund-management companies love bandwagons. They see that a sector, a stock market or an asset has performed very well over the past 6 or 12 months, so they launch a fund to market that flavour.

✔ Claiming a fund is the top or best of something even if it's the fund-management equivalent of best marrow at the local gardeners' show. So you get publicity like 'the top quartile in its sector over three years'. Note that marketing people love quartiles, where you divide a list into four. If publicity misses out on a 'top quartile' showing, then you can bet that the past performance was rubbish.

✔ Boasting about awards from investment trade publications. The thing is, so many categories exist that almost everyone gets a prize. There are even prizes for best administration or adviser service, which means these firms are fastest with commission cheques. Anyway, these awards are dished out, so managers dress up and show up at £250-a-head award dinners where they can drink themselves stupid and be entertained for 20 minutes by a TV comic (who picks up £20,000 for the gig).

- ✔ Pushing optimism and relegating any thought the fund could lose to the statutory small print.

- ✔ Playing the percentages: fund managers might go for a high-risk strategy so if they get it right, they can boast about it, and if all goes wrong, they can hide the fund and get on with marketing another.

- ✔ Taking media-friendly independent financial advisers for a few golfing afternoons so they'll praise the products the next time a journalist calls for a quote or sound bite.

- ✔ Taking journalists on all-expenses-paid trips to exotic places, such as South Africa, Morocco and Hong Kong, with business class travel and five-star hotels. That guarantees acres of favourable coverage.

Am I being excessively cynical? The investment industry would say I am. But always remember you can't take an investment back to the shop because you don't like it once you get home. So be a savvy investor by watching out for marketing tricks.

Evaluating the Worth of Performance Tables

One of the most controversial issues in fund management is past performance and whether it has any relationship to the future. Academics have said that you have as much chance of picking a future winning fund by selecting the best from the past as you have of winning at roulette by looking at where the balls ended up earlier.

The FSA has said that the past has no serious predictive value. At one time the FSA wanted to ban past-performance figures because the FSA said they just confuse investors. But the fund-management industry put up a spirited defence of the practice (without which it would have to rewrite most of its adverts), and its view has prevailed.

Whether your collective is an investment trust, unit trust or insurance bond, performance tables are available for you to scrutinise. The tables are subdivided into sectors, such as UK bonds or Pacific equities excluding Japan. The idea of sector tables is to compare apples with apples, not oranges or pears.

Tables used to be published once a month and then a month in arrears. Now you can easily find up-to-date figures on websites such as Trustnet (www.trustnet.co.uk) or Morningstar (www.morningstar.co.uk). These allow you to sort funds according to your criteria, such as time periods so you can see which ones have done well over ten years or over just one month.

Keep in mind, though, that comparisons don't always work that smoothly. Some funds are mobile. They move their asset mix over time and change sectors, usually to make the collective look better.

When examining performance tables, which are subdivided into sectors, keep in mind that coming in fifth in a sector of 200 is a real achievement, but coming in fifth in a sector of 10 is just average.

The ideal collective isn't one that's currently topping the table. Too many fund managers have succeeded in heading the league one day and propping it up by the time you've bought into it. Instead, look for consistency over the years. The fund that generally beats 60 or 70 per cent of its competitors on a regular basis is the one to aim for. If past performance shows anything, it's that managers who are consistently ahead of the majority provide better value for investors than those with flash-in-the-pan genius followed by down-the-pan disaster.

The same figures can tell different stories

All tables assume that you start off with a set amount (usually £1,000) and reinvest any dividends after any tax over a variety of time periods. But after that, they can show two quite different scenarios. Most tables are cumulative so you see what you would've got after, say, five years. Ones that show discrete performance can tell a different story.

Cumulative tables give no idea of consistency. The good or bad performance may have been due to one great or one atrocious patch nearly five years ago. Going down to the three- or one-year tables may show the fund manager in a different light altogether. A fund may show that it doubled over ten years. But scratch that a bit, and you'll see that it tripled during its first year and then lost money ever since! The reason may be due to a change of manager, a change of style from risky to cautious or vice versa or, most likely, a change of market conditions. Some fund managers work best in fast-rising markets; others shine when stock markets are less alluring.

So if you want to judge consistency and filter out one period of amazing good (or bad) decision-making, go for the discrete figures (see the following section for more info).

Tables that use discrete figures

Discrete-figure tables show every single year (or three- or six-month periods if you wish) for the past five or ten years, so you see the results for a number of 12-month periods taken individually. If your table were dated June 2010, for example, you'd have the 12 months from 1 June 2009 to 31 May 2010, as well as the year from 1 June 2008 to 31 May 2009, and so on.

Discrete figures let you judge consistency and when the out- or under-performance occurred. A fund with a ten-year cumulative performance that was superb eight, nine and ten years ago and then reverted to a little below average would still look good over ten years. But the discrete figures would expose its less than inspiring performance since.

Discrete-period tables are a powerful past-performance tool that most marketing departments would rather you didn't see. In print, the easiest place to find them is in *Money Management* magazine, a monthly publication available at newsagents. It's read by both serious investors and the packaged-investment trade. Over longer periods the tortoise beats the hare.

Get savvy with fund performance-table talk

A *quartile* means that a table has been divided into four subsections. First-quartile performance is the top 25 per cent of the table, which may be anything from a few funds to more than 100. Anything from average upward appears in the top two quartiles. Third and fourth quartiles are for the also-rans.

A *decile* means that a table has been divided into ten subsections. The top decile of a table of 100 funds is the first 10. So top decile is better than top quartile, and bottom decile is worse than bottom quartile. Avoid funds in the bottom two deciles like the plague.

What tables are strongest at showing

Past performance is most accurate in predicting really bad fund managers. Collectives that have spent most of their life in investment's equivalent of the fourth division relegation zone tend to stay there. You can use this info to eliminate the no-hopers. Good funds may go down, and average funds may go up. But rarely does the total rubbish ever throw off that poor-performance mantle and shine.

Appreciating the Worth of Fund-Manager Fees

The collective-fund industry would rather not focus on costs. Instead, it'd prefer to concentrate on benefits. But you can't separate the two. Whatever gains professional management may bring, you may lose them, and then some more, if you pay too much in fees.

The costs of buying into a fund aren't too much of a problem – and as you'll see later on in this chapter, you can avoid them either completely or largely by signing up to a fund supermarket. But these fees aren't that different from those involved with purchasing individual shares. You generally aren't charged an exit fee from a unit trust (or an insurance fund, although few people now buy these because they only appeal to people with specialist tax needs) so think of the initial charge as a round-trip in-and-out fee. Many independent financial advisers, known as discount brokers, rebate part of the upfront fee.

Annual fees are where you're often hit hard. These fees are often shown at 1.5 per cent, but the counting doesn't stop there. Fund fees attract VAT (value added tax), making the real figure nearer to 1.75 per cent. Add on some compounding and, in rough terms, a fund held for ten years would give its managers around 20 per cent of your money, or about 9 per cent over five years. But some tracker funds can charge as little as 0.3 per cent each year.

To show value, a high-cost fund manager must add more than 20 per cent to a ten-year investment and around 10 per cent to a five-year holding for the holder to break even. Managers who can consistently deliver good results with the costs handicap can congratulate themselves. Frequent traders are harder hit by entry costs.

Filling Your Financial Trolley at Fund Supermarkets

Buying from a fund supermarket is little different from other online shopping experiences. You choose what you want, put the items in your trolley and pay at the checkout. And you'd expect to pay less than going to the old-fashioned store. Except, the sums involved here are going to be bigger than your usual grocery bill. In general, you pay nothing or very little upfront. If you go to a traditional adviser or broker – or if you buy directly from the investment company itself – you typically lose around 5 per cent of each investment in upfront charges.

Fund supermarkets typically offer around 1,500 unit trusts, which is enough for almost everyone. And after you've signed up to a supermarket – you could join more than one but the complications probably outweigh any greater choice – you can register all your existing holdings of similar funds as well. That gives a one-stop shop where you can see what you have and track your purchases, sales and dividends. Having everything in one place can be useful when it comes to filling in your self-assessment tax form. Look for 'consolidation' on the site. This tells you that you can list all your applicable investments.

What does the site get out of this? Unit trusts pay something called *trail commission*. This isn't a payment for going on a long-distance walk but an annual amount – usually 0.5 per cent of the value of the holding – which can be paid to the supermarket or to the independent financial adviser whose name might appear on it. It's one of the confusions of the supermarket that some are labelled either with their own name or with that of an adviser. Think of own-brand drinks at the real supermarket – they're all made by companies that also manufacture under different brands.

Fund supermarkets don't tell you what to buy. But they offer a whole range of tools such as tables and easy access to the investment firm's own website, where you'll find 'fact sheets'. These are really aimed at the professional broker but you'll find a whole range of useful information including statements from the managers and a list of the larger holdings in the portfolio.

The two totally dominant supermarkets are operated by Fidelity Funds (www.fundsnetwork.co.uk) and Co-funds (www.cofunds.co.uk). Some discount brokers let you opt for one or the other – others tell you which one to have. Where you have a choice try both out, but it'll probably make no difference to your future wealth. Again, it's like food supermarkets, where you select one for regular use on factors such as convenience, layout and parking.

Don't go straight to a supermarket if you really want hand-holding advice. But don't be surprised if after a broker has created a portfolio for you, it ends up in a supermarket environment. It's just that it's much simpler to administer this way.

Chapter 13

Hedging Your Fund Bets

● ●

In This Chapter

▶ Understanding what hedge funds are

▶ Understanding the strategies that are available

▶ Knowing about some new ideas based on hedge funds

● ●

*T*he reputation of hedge funds is appalling. I can't put it a nicer way. It's bad, terrible, dreadful. People blame hedge funds for almost everything, from the collapse of banks to the collapse of currencies to the collapse of jobs. And I've probably left out a few collapses. Additionally, many are unregulated and offshore, or if they're subject to a rulebook, it's a very slim one.

But although many make huge sums for their managers and investors, many also fail. You hear a lot less about the duds than the stellar performers. Hedge funds are very risky and about as far as you can get from a one-way bet to riches.

So why look at hedge funds then? The simple fact is that you can't ignore them. They wield enormous market power; they can be either very successful or so dangerous they risk bringing down the system – as they did with their attack on the UK banks a few years ago. But more importantly, recent changes in legislation mean hedge funds (or funds run on a similar basis) are increasingly available to investors outside the millionaire bracket. One increasingly popular mainstream form of collective is the absolute-return fund that I describe later in this chapter. At the same time, your pension fund may invest in hedge funds, so it's a good idea to know how they work. Additionally, many investment trusts, including those aimed at savers investing perhaps £100 a month, now feature hedge funds in their portfolios. So your future fortune may be riding on one of these funds without your knowledge. They're the genie that you can't force back into the bottle.

For all these reasons, you need to know about hedge funds and how they work, even if you can't or don't want to invest in them. Most people won't take their money to these funds, but knowing how they operate helps you better understand what's going on – and perhaps gives you some tactics that you can use. That's where this chapter comes in.

Defining Hedge Funds

Hedge funds – sometimes (and confusingly) called alternative investments even though they have nothing in common with old-style alternatives such as classic cars or stamp collections – have been around since the late 1940s. Literally tens of thousands of them exist around the globe. No one knows quite how many of them are actually out there because there's no listing everyone agrees on. And new ones are born and failures die every year.

Strictly speaking, the term *hedge fund* only refers to a specialised legal structure. Hedge funds are private-partnership contracts where the manager has a substantial personal interest in the fund and is free to operate in a variety of markets using a number of strategies. It's best to think of a hedge fund as giving investors' money to a manager who has unfettered freedom to invest in areas other funds can't reach. These freedoms include the ability to

- ✔ Be flexible. Most hedge-fund managers can do what they like within wide parameters. They're not restricted by trust deeds to a narrow range of equities or bonds like other collectives, although a few have stated strategies that limit what they can do in financial markets.

- ✔ Go short. Ordinary fund managers only select shares they think will do well and hence go up, a technique known as *going long*. Hedge-fund managers can also choose equities they think will sink, making money as the shares fall, a technique known as *going short* or *short selling*. If hedge-fund managers see a company in serious trouble, they can take a one-way bet on the shares going down to zero. When other investors see hedge funds attacking the company in this way, they sell as well, putting extra pressure on the share price.

✔ Employ derivatives, such as futures, options and some very exotic bets on interest rates, currencies and even *volatility*, which is the speed with which an investment moves up or down. Stacks of strategies exist here – enough to fill a whole shelf with *For Dummies* books on them.

✔ Move in and out of cash, currencies, commodities, gold and property as well as other investments at high speed.

✔ Use borrowings (known as *gearing* in the UK and *leverage* in the United States) in an aggressive fashion to improve returns. Of course, if they get it wrong, then borrowing works against them.

You can only access hedge funds via a stockbroker or other regulated professional adviser. Getting information on funds can be difficult because most are secretive, and many of them operate out of tax havens where corporate governance rules are lax. Whatever you're advised to do, always check that you're happy with the management firm and where it's based before considering moving a penny in their direction. Hedge funds can and do disappear.

Choosing Strategies

Broadly speaking, hedge funds fall into categories. Firstly, every hedge fund exists either to maximise returns or to offer a safe haven while trying to return more than an investor would get from leaving his or her money in cash deposits at the bank. Around half of all funds are run on a long–short strategy (see the section 'Opportunistic strategies' for the details). Beyond that, eight other well-defined strategies are available for managers to pursue. These strategies come under three main headings: relative value, event driven and opportunistic.

Relative-value strategies

This tactic is at the lower-risk end of the hedge-fund spectrum because it doesn't depend on whether or not the market is enthusiastic for oil companies or banks or food producers or automotive engineers, just on the relative values of two closely connected stock-market investments such as two banks or two oil companies. This is because the factors affecting one company in a sector are similar to those affecting a competitor company, especially over the short term. But the factors aren't so similar as to be the same.

With relative-value strategies, the hedge fund tries to profit from price gaps between the same or similar investments in different markets. For instance, some shares are quoted and traded on more than one stock market. Minor differences between the two might exist, often only available for a minute or so, as local prices react to something happening in another country, or because the local stock market is more enthusiastic (or less keen) on shares themselves that day. Three main types of relative-value fund are available:

- ✔ **Convertible arbitrage:** Some shares have convertible bonds as well as conventional shares. Exploiting price differences can be profitable.

- ✔ **Fixed-income arbitrage:** This one is for the rocket scientists who try to make money by buying and selling bonds with the same credit risk (so they stick to UK gilts or US treasuries) but with different maturity dates or different headline interest rates.

- ✔ **Equity market neutral:** Traditional collective-fund managers try to find shares that will go up, but equity-neutral managers aren't concerned with the direction of markets or shares. Instead, they look for differences between shares and derivatives, so they may sell a bank share but buy a bank-based derivative. Another route is to sell overvalued shares and buy undervalued shares. It's up to the managers to decide which are overvalued and which undervalued – no flags are flying here.

Event-driven strategies

This tactic focuses on shares in companies that are involved in takeovers, acquisitions and other forms of corporate restructuring. Big rewards await those who get this strategy right, and huge losses occur if all goes wrong.

Here are the main types of event-driven strategies:

✔ **Merger arbitrage:** This type concentrates on companies that are either acquiring or being acquired through
takeovers. The shares often have a life of their own, independent of general market forces. Hedge-fund managers
using this tactic hope to make money out of the fears of
other investors that the deal will be scuppered by other
shareholders or government regulators.

✔ **Distressed securities:** Here, managers try to make money
from equities and bonds on the verge of collapse. Some
hedge-fund managers end up with significant stakes
in the company concerned, so they can influence any
rescue attempt. Sometimes, the hedge fund wants the
company to collapse to maximise its strategy. Because
the hedge fund looks to the short term, it's probably not
interested in long-term reconstruction attempts.

Opportunistic strategies

These are the riskiest hedge-fund strategies, promising high
returns or threatening big losses. The hedge-fund managers
bet on stock-market directions – up, down or sideways. But
they can also invest in other areas, such as commodities,
bonds and currencies.

Here are the main types of opportunistic strategies:

✔ **Long–short:** This is the big one, accounting for about
half of all hedge-fund activity. The idea is that expert
managers (often with a track record in equities or bonds
elsewhere) aim for positive returns from a small portfolio of shares in companies they know well by either
selling them (going short) if they think the price will
fall or buying them (going long) as they see fit. Some go
for more complicated tactics such as buying what they
consider to be the best share in a sector and selling the
weakest. So they sell the worst (in their opinion) oil company, for example, and buy the best. Or vice versa.

Short selling usually involves shares that the fund never
owned. Techniques to exploit price falls are more complicated than those used to gain from rising prices.

✔ **Macro:** With this tactic, the managers take bets on big worldwide movements in all sorts of markets but especially those where their activities are hidden by huge amounts of trading by others. They hope to second-guess market moves.

✔ **Short selling:** This type specialises in techniques to make money out of falling equity and bond values. It's a very high-risk tactic. If the investment moves the other way, the losses can be massive. Purchasers of shares who hope the price will rise can only lose their stake if the asset falls to zero. Now suppose that you sell a share with a £1 price, hoping to buy it back later at 50p and take out 50p a share profit, but you get it wrong. That share could soar to £2, £5 or who knows how high. So short sellers face limitless losses. And when markets are rising steeply, short-selling funds have to stay on the sidelines.

✔ **Emerging markets:** This type is really for the ultra-courageous. These are the riskiest hedge funds because they invest in less well-developed markets where information is sketchy, legal and administrative systems are often unstable, local politics are volatile, and the companies themselves are often run by managers who either lack experience or are corrupt. Most investors run a mile from this type. But hedge-fund managers see it as an opportunity, trying to profit from the very problems that scare off others.

Taking Hedging Some Stages Further

The big advantage of hedge funds is that they can make money when share prices fall as well as when they rise. But, if the truth be told, many investors are scared of hedge funds or think they're only for those with hundreds of thousands, if not millions, spare. So mainstream investment companies, such as unit-trust management firms, have come up with some new ideas based on hedge-fund thinking, but not carrying that label, and accessible to investors with relatively small sums. Many start at £5,000 and some will take as little as £1,000.

Only look at these fund ideas if you're experienced and able to withstand periods of losses. They're not intended for the first-time investor. Always check on how the managers intend to reward themselves. Some have been known to prioritise their own remuneration before that of their investors, so be careful.

Absolute-return funds offer a kind of 'hedge funds lite'. Aimed at the private investor, they use many of the hedge-fund techniques listed in the previous sections, but in a UK-regulated fund. Their numbers have grown substantially with many investors attracted by their aim of gaining in both rising and falling markets.

Absolute-return funds are hedge funds in all but name. Their managers operate a flexible strategy: they can borrow, *sell short* (sell stocks they don't have) and go into futures, options and almost anything else they can think of to enhance their returns. Some adopt a strategy known as *market neutral*, where most of the fund aims to match the stock market, leaving a small proportion over for a handful of investments that the managers expect to rise substantially in price.

Their aim is to give a better return than cash in the bank but minimise the risks involved in big one-way bets on equities or bonds where managers hope to make relative returns (that's relative to each other and not to any other investor requirement). But absolute return tries to give you gains over and above a set benchmark such as what you'd get from a bank account.

Why have the funds become so popular? Here are three reasons:

- ✔ They're still new; only recently did the watchdog – the Financial Services Authority – give the legal go-ahead to sell them to the public. Before then, funds could only buy shares in the hope of rises.

- ✔ No one can pretend the first decade of this century was a good time for equities – unlike the 1980s and 1990s. As a result, investors are now wary of claims that managers can make money – too many have lost out.

- ✔ People hope that something new can win out over strategies that have effectively flopped.

Making gains is far harder in a low-inflation, low-interest-rate environment. So absolute-return funds set their sights lower than relative return – and they're not afraid to put all or a large part of the portfolio in cash if other assets are uncertain.

So do these funds deliver what they say on the tin?

Most absolute-return funds are still wet behind the ears at the time of writing, so the jury will be out for some time on whether they work or not. Managers stress that investors shouldn't expect the funds to make money every single month. Instead, you must judge them over a five- to ten-year period during which almost anything can happen.

Absolute-return funds tend to charge higher fees than relative-return funds, so managers will have to justify their high earnings. You pay annual fees plus a performance-related fee, which is usually high.

The performance part should be charged on the amount a fund produces over and above a minimum level. Check that any fund you invest in has a high-water mark. This means that if a fund falls, it has to make up the losses and get back to where it was before it can charge again. Always check this high-water mark to see where it is. Some funds have been known to use cheeky tricks to move it down so that the managers earn more.

Most absolute-return funds aim to be cautiously managed, so if a fund screams 'exceptional returns' then it's likely the managers have taken big risks.

Don't expect absolute-return funds to shine if equities are soaring ahead. The higher that percentage, the greater the potential rewards but also the larger the possible risks. A fund advertising itself as cash plus 5 to 7 per cent would be higher up the risk ladder than a fund offering 2 to 3 per cent over the cash return. The first would appeal to adventurous investors; the second to more cautious savers.

Making money from yo-yo asset prices

How do you make money if interest rates stay stubbornly low and share prices end each year roughly at the same level they started? The answer to that problem could be to play *volatility*. This is a bet on whether short-term movements will be sharply up or down, or whether they'll show little difference day in, day out.

Volatility ignores whether markets are rising or falling. It's the speed and intensity of each move that counts. Investors usually concentrate on market indexes rather than individual equities, so if the Standard & Poor's index of US shares moves up 10 per cent one day and down 10 per cent the next, that's greater volatility than if it moved up 0.1 per cent and then down 0.1 per cent. Of course, in both instances the market is almost unchanged over two days. (The *almost* is because a percentage up and then the same down doesn't bring you back to zero.)

Think of a yo-yo. When it's working well, the ups and downs are substantial even though you end up in much the same place.

The most used measure of volatility is the VIX index. Investors can go for greater or lesser volatility with a number of strategies.

Some Do's and Don'ts: A Hedge-Fund Checklist

Because very few investors other than the ultra-rich have ever bought into a hedge fund, and because hedge funds are rarely mentioned in the press, precious little help and advice is immediately on hand for the average investor. So you have to tread very carefully. Here are the basic do's and don'ts:

✔ Do ensure that a fund of funds manager reveals their standards for selecting and monitoring hedge-fund managers.

✔ Don't let hedge funds hold more than a limited place in your portfolio. Most advisers say to limit them to 10 per cent of the portfolio's total value.

✔ Do check that the adviser or broker understands hedge funds and is up to date with information on them.

✔ Do always be sure that you know about fees and charges. They can be significant and erode stated gains.

✔ Don't invest if you're in doubt about a hedge fund or a fund of hedge funds. Hedge funds and your cash make a highly volatile mix, so if you're in doubt, just don't do it.

Chapter 14

Investing at Random and with the Intellectuals

*D*on't worry about the heading of this chapter. You don't have to have worked through Aristotle or Einstein or Freud, or worried about the point of life with the French writers of the 1950s (although *Existentialism For Dummies* is a really good read). Instead, this chapter looks at how some of the leading investment brains in the world view the subject and what you can do with their knowledge.

You don't have to follow these intellectuals' thoughts. But you do need to know what they think so you can better understand the investment process and how it affects your savings. It doesn't matter whether these theories are right or wrong now. They'll have been right at some stage and they have a huge influence on the way professional money managers move their billions. And what these money managers do sets the scene for what you can achieve.

This chapter starts on a subject most investors have been conditioned to believe is pure fiction. It's not. It's about how you can perform as well as the average fund manager or stockbroker using no technology more complicated than a pin. I used my own children as guinea pigs in this. (Don't worry: my kids were old enough to handle a pin, and no animals were harmed in the videoing.)

Pinning Your Hopes on Chance

One of my all-time favourite investment books is *A Random Walk Down Wall Street* (WW Norton, 1973) by US writer Burton Malkiel. The book was first published in the early '70s, and since then it's been updated at least eight times and has been constantly in print. Much of the book is high-flown investment theory, but Malkiel also describes the most devastating puncturing of the postures of highly paid experts.

You can do as well as most professionals with nothing more complex than a pin and a list of shares. Back in June 1967, bored journalists on US investment magazine *Forbes* were sitting around in their New York office, discussing the way top fund managers produced results that ranged from marvellous to miserable each year and the way that a manager who did well one or two years in a row rarely made that three or four. In fact, over five years, only a tiny handful managed to perform consistently well. This remains true to this day. A Wall Street contact had joked that a blindfolded monkey stabbing a share price page with a pin could do as well as some of the chumps working for big fund groups. So they decided to test the theory, which is now known as the Random Walk. The rest is history. Tested and tested again in subsequent years, the pin beat most of the professionals – even more so because the pin, unlike the experts, cost nothing!

In the 1990s I regularly featured a New Year portfolio with a pin (selected by my then small children, Zoe and Oliver, from the share price pages in the *Financial Times*). It started as an antidote to those New Year share prediction articles, which promised to foretell the future but probably only wrote up shares already held by the writers' sources.

Most years, the portfolio selected by my offspring outperformed the average UK fund manager; one year it was in the top 5 per cent and did better than all the professional newspaper tipster columns. Okay, on two occasions out of the ten times we did this, it fell below the average, but not disastrously. The results were third quartile rather than bottom of the fourth division.

Why did I stop? The newspaper I used to write for shut down its business pages. (Nothing to do with my contribution, well, unless it was my scepticism that led to a dearth of fund-manager adverts.)

Knowing the Limits of a Random-Choice Portfolio

The pin is a pretty good investment-choice tool, but it's not all powerful. It's not a guarantee against losses. No collective manager can insulate against a falling stock market, and neither can the random-choice-method investor.

You need a long time span

You need time and patience for a random-choice approach to work. Remember that doing nothing for ten years is worth a lot. In rough terms, investing £10,000 into a market that doubles would give you about £19,700 after a decade of doing nothing. The £300 loss is down to purchase costs and stamp duty. In comparison, with an active fund manager taking 1.5 per cent (plus VAT in many instances) annual fees plus internal costs of dealing in and out of shares, you'd be lucky to have £17,000.

Paid-for managers would have to be really on the ball to overcome that cost handicap. A minority of them manage to do so. A few do even better. The problem is that you don't know which funds will succeed and which will fail, but the failures always outnumber the winners over time.

Note that if a market stood still for ten years, your buy-and-hold portfolio would be worth about £9,700 after costs. The same investment with a high-cost collective manager would go down to just over £8,500. (All these figures ignore dividends, by the way. Dividends really boost your fortune if you reinvest them. Remember that active fund managers grab about half or more of your dividend to pay for their champagne lifestyle.)

A compromise route for equities is to diversify and split your share cash – investing half via whatever the pin lands on and half into a low-cost global growth investment trust. Some very low-cost lump-sum investment and regular savings schemes are on offer. Look at the Association of Investment Companies website (www.theaic.co.uk) for further details.

Diversification is the posh way of saying you don't put all your investment eggs in one basket. It's been a mainstay of investing thinking for decades. Everyone – including me – has stressed that you need to spread out your savings across a wide variety of asset classes before you even start dividing your money up between individual shares, bonds or funds. The idea has always been that each asset class is 'uncorrelated' with any other. So what happens in the property market doesn't have any relationship with what's going on in shares or bonds or currencies.

Traditionally, you need to select assets

The toughest take in any investment decision has always been to select your asset classes. You have to decide what proportion of your money you want to go where. (And if you've read the stuff about Random Walks in the earlier section 'Pinning Your Hopes on Chance', prepare to put your pin away. You can't select asset classes in this way.)

The basic advice has always been that you need to allocate your savings between these big-picture items:

- ✔ Equities
- ✔ Bonds
- ✔ Property
- ✔ Cash

Although you can choose to ignore foreign holdings, bond and equity purchasers may have to fine-tune between UK and overseas, which may involve foreign currencies. Only after you've made this allocation decision can you get down to fine-tuning your holdings. You first have to decide that, perhaps, 35 per cent of your money should be held in bonds before working out which bonds or bond funds to buy.

Understanding Modern Portfolio Theory

Diversification is based on something called Modern Portfolio Theory (MPT for short). Volumes upon volumes are devoted to the theory. Some of it is really, really difficult to understand, but you don't need a doctorate in investment science or even a spreadsheet to get the basics.

First, know that MPT isn't actually modern any more. It was first invented by Harry Markowitz in an economics dissertation for his doctorate degree at Chicago University in 1952. Markowitz incidentally went on to win a Nobel Prize in 1990, so his thinking wasn't a one-day wonder.

MPT starts off with the assumption that investors aren't wild speculators or saloon bar gamblers. They want returns, but want to avoid risk as far as they can, although they know all life has some risks. (After all, leaving cash under the mattress risks fire, vermin and theft, and it earns nothing.) And regarding their return, most investors are content to aim somewhere near the average.

Traditional investors focus on analysing each component share or bond in a portfolio. They prefer Bank A to Bank B because they like the former's chief executive, or they prefer Oil Company C to Oil Company D because the latter is involved in exploration in an expensive (and unlikely to produce) area.

Now for the really clever bit, according to MPT followers. Instead of looking at the risks in individual stocks, you measure how they all react with each other and calculate the overall risks inherent in your portfolio. MPT says that you can then get a higher return from the whole thing compared with the risk of each component stock. Using something called the *efficient frontier*, you can build a portfolio that maximises the return while minimising the risk.

So instead of looking at companies like a traditional fund manager from a business point of view, including factors such as management, profits and prospects, you look at how a share moves up and down in relationship to the market as a whole and to the other holdings in the portfolio.

MPT goes beyond the individual risk and looks at the overall risks in the portfolio. The idea is to see how portfolio components react or correlate with each other. For example, a hot weather spell is good for breweries. People drink more beer when it's warm. A hot weather spell is bad for gas sales because central heating is turned off. So brewery shares rise and gas producer stocks fall. And in a cold spell, the sums work in the opposite direction. So it's like a see-saw with the weather playing a big part in deciding what's up and what's down. But by owning both beer producers and gas companies, you've reduced the risk of being hit by unexpected weather.

Now suppose your portfolio consists of a warm outdoors coat company and a heating-oil firm. If the winter weather is unexpectedly cold, both companies will do well because they're correlated. But if December, January and February are unexpectedly mild, both will do badly. You've spread your holdings but in a way that the risk – the weather here – will impact either very positively or very badly.

High oil prices are good for fuel companies but bad for airlines, which need to stock up with their products. Here again, there's a low correlation. So a portfolio is better diversified against the unexpected by having one brewery, one gas company, one fuel firm and one airline than by having four banks or four of anything else.

MPT needs time to work. It's like an insurance company. In a bad weather spell that may only last a day, an insurance company will lose money to flood and tornado claims. The company also knows that wooden homes are a greater fire hazard than those built of brick. So it has lots of risks. But although each policy may represent a huge loss, the insurance company knows that if it gets its maths and customer mix right, it will make some money for its owners over time.

It's all to do with making your portfolio a safer place to be – anyone can take wild gambles, but do you really want to do this with your life's savings or your pension money?

If you can get the mix right, then you've reached MPT's nirvana – the efficient market frontier.

MPT assumes that investors want to minimise risks and not take wild punts. It doesn't work well among the penny dreadfuls or tipsheet favourites, where small-investor hope and greed overcome reason and moderation.

Exploring the Hybrid Portfolio Theory

Now for the anti-modern case that's so new you could easily call it Post-post-modern Portfolio Theory.

Those who go against MPT (see the previous section) – the anti-MPTers, as they call themselves – start out with an idea that investors want safety of what they have first, the ability to get at that money second, an income flow third and finally the promise of capital appreciation.

This is hardly revolutionary or rocket science. It lists the priorities that form the basis of this book. And because the anti-MPT line has only started to gain publicity since the very first edition of this book, perhaps they read it first!

The anti-MPTers point to the half-dozen big stock-market shocks over the past 25 years and say it's time for investors to rethink their approach. And what they've come up with is Hybrid Portfolio Theory (HPT). This is so new that probably 99 per cent of investment professionals have never heard of it. So you'll be one up on them.

The portfolio divisions

As an HPT investor, you divide your entire savings into two distinct (hybrid) portfolios.

The larger portfolio (A) represents 75 to 90 per cent of the assets, and you invest this with the primary objective of liquidity (the ease with which you can recover your money), safety of principal (the money itself) and income. This portfolio is an as-near-safe-as-you-can-get mix of risk-free and short-term money market instruments and bonds. So this portfolio has to maximise income but only to the point where the holder feels secure.

You could leave it all in a bank deposit account. More likely, you invest all of this part of your money – don't forget it's by far the biggest section of your personal wealth – into inflation-proofed UK government bonds. You see most of the rest of the bond market as too risky.

One big advantage of this approach is that you don't have to pay big management charges because the range of super-safe assets is narrow so there's not much choice.

What's left after you invest in portfolio A goes into what HPTers call portfolio B, which is designed to generate growth. This is the risk element that's designed to give your assets a big push into future growth. You typically put this into equities, with a fair slice at the higher-risk end of the spectrum. So you might get an exposure to emerging markets or even frontier markets (*frontier markets* are those where outside or international investors have so far been reluctant to try their luck – think Cambodia rather than China, or Tanzania rather than Thailand).

Investors adjust the balance according to their needs. Anyone close to retirement would go to the higher end of Portfolio A – around 95 per cent, leaving little to risk. Someone who's unlikely to need to spend the money for a decade or two or more can go for a higher percentage in the risk section – that's Portfolio B.

Will HPT work?

Investors who follow this HPT concept do less well when risky assets are booming (as they did in the 1990s) but better when shares are in the doldrums (for most of the first decade of this century) because the vast majority of assets aren't exposed to a downright bad wager relative to risk-free or short-term assets. And it cuts the risk of unpredictable (yet, frequent) black swan events, which ruin portfolios that have taken a lifetime to construct.

But the approach is so new, no one knows how it works long term. It could be the solution for investors who are fed up with the way they have to pay for advice and strategies that leave them as poor as when they started. And the anti-MPTers say it's got more chance than some of the discredited ideas peddled previously.

Investing the great bulk of your money into safe assets goes against the grain of the past 60 or so, years when the mantra of shares, shares, shares was dominant. But if you return to the low-inflation times of previous generations, then it will be far more difficult for equities to outperform overall.

Part IV
Property and Alternatives

In this part . . .

*T*he biggest investment most people ever make is in property – their own. The running costs of the roof over your head plus the expense of paying off the mortgage each month eat up a large part of most people's earnings. As a result, many people only start serious investment after they've paid off their mortgage. In a low-inflation environment, it makes sense to get shot of the home loan as quickly as possible. Rising property prices won't come riding to your rescue as they once did.

But this part looks at going one stage further than just buying a property to live in. Property as an investment has been a neglected asset in the UK. But with many financial markets taking on an uncertain air, putting money into what you can see can be a worthwhile, lower-risk route for your savings. So this part goes through the pros and cons of getting into bricks and mortar as an investment. Buy-to-let residential property has come – and certainly gone – in its get-rich-quick form. And investing in commercial property, such as office blocks and shopping centres, is also an option, especially for long-term pension funds.

In addition to covering property investments, this part looks at alternative investments. I'm not talking about old-fashioned alternatives, like wine or vintage cars. I'm talking about a new style of alternatives, like spread bets, hedge funds and traded options. Alternatives are becoming more and more publicised, so you need to know about them, but consider yourself duly warned up front: they're an avenue in which you can literally lose not just your shirt but everything else you own.

Chapter 15

Investing in Bricks and Mortar

*B*uy-to-let was the fastest growing investment class in the UK during most of the first decade of this century. From being virtually non-existent in the mid-1990s it grew, along with prices for houses and flats, to more than rival many collective investment schemes. However, buy-to-let enthusiasts forgot – or probably had never heard of – the number one investment rule: nothing is a one-way bet. They convinced themselves that buy-to-let couldn't fail; that both property values and rents would always rise. They also forgot not to place too much of their future in an investment that could be difficult, time consuming and costly to sell. Property isn't liquid like shares or bonds or cash at the bank.

However, none of this should stop residential property investment. If you're careful, this investing can provide a useful extra income over the years. But the days of instant fortunes and dinner party boasting are over.

This chapter gives you the need-to-know basics about investing in a buy-to-let property – the pros and cons as well as the mortgage, location, tenant and tax issues. In addition, this chapter introduces you to investing in commercial property, in case you want to go down that route.

Buying Property to Rent: The Pros and Cons

Buying to let involves buying a second (or third or fourth or sometimes even more) property in addition to the one you live in yourself. You rent this extra home to a tenant, and if all goes well, you earn rent once a month and see your initial capital investment rise as well. You gain an income and increase your wealth at the same time. That's the theory, and it can work in practice, providing your expectations are modest, your time horizon is long and you do your homework.

The popularity of buy-to-let grew because

- ✔ Investors were fed up with shares that don't deliver.
- ✔ Investors wanted an investment with a solid feel.
- ✔ Investors were looking for an investment they could get involved in.
- ✔ Investors didn't want to be tied to expensive fund managers who fail to perform.
- ✔ The whole idea appealed to many people who wanted to operate their own spare-time business.
- ✔ Mobile people always need somewhere to live but don't want to buy a property that they may have to quit at short notice.
- ✔ Property prices in some areas remain out of reach of first-time buyers. Because they must live somewhere, they rent.
- ✔ Interest rates for borrowers have become very low. And although mortgage firms are choosy about what they will lend upon, they now see this activity as mainstream and no longer charge a huge interest-rate premium for buy-to-let loans.
- ✔ Estate agents set up units to deal with rented property.

✔ It's far easier to borrow in order to purchase a property to rent even if you still owe money on your original residence than it once was.

You may have noticed that some of the reasons are in the past tense and others are in the present. That's because the past tense ones aren't as certain as they once seemed to be. The first decade of this century was largely dominated by property. Who knows if that will remain true for the years up to 2020? Or will shares return? Only you as an individual can judge. After all, property is a long-term purchase, but you can move in and out of shares in the blink of an eye.

Buy-to-let isn't guaranteed. You may find yourself without a tenant, and you may lose money on the property because prices can fall as well as rise. Or, you could find that your tenant refuses to pay and trashes the place upon leaving (and, by the way, unless you have insurance to cover bad tenants, you could spend thousands in legal fees evicting people whom you don't like).

Some other potential drawbacks exist as well:

✔ You can't get your money out in a hurry. Selling a property may take a year or longer, especially if house price rises stall or go into reverse. If you need to sell in a hurry, you'll probably have to accept less.

✔ You need to be hands on, even if you employ an agent to deal with tenants.

✔ Getting a portfolio of properties is very expensive. Most buy-to-letters just have one property, so there's no diversification. It's even worse if you put all your spare cash into this one property.

A move into buy-to-let is far bigger than any move into equities, bonds or cash. You can't change your mind in a few minutes or even a few months' time. You may also have to do all the work yourself, including checking and cleaning the property between tenants, or if that sounds awful then you'll have to pay at least 15 per cent of the rent to have someone else manage the property.

Before considering affordability or whether buy-to-let is the right type of investment for your needs, use the negative points of buy-to-let as a checklist to see whether the idea even appeals to you.

Considering Affordability

Very few buy-to-let investors can afford to pay cash for their property purchase even though in some (admittedly not too desirable) locations, flats and houses can still cost under £50,000 especially if you buy *distressed* properties at auction (those that need some repair work before you can legally rent them out).

But even if you could afford to pay cash, you should never tie up so much of your capital in a property that it leaves you without an emergency fund or the ability to buy into other investment assets if you think the time is right. So most buy-to-let investors borrow money either out of necessity or to balance their portfolios better.

The price you see or even agree to isn't the property's real price. You also have to pay for stamp duty, which is levied as a percentage of the purchase price – the more expensive the property, the higher the percentage. Stamp-duty rates have varied over the past few years as governments try to encourage first-time buyers (that's not you as a buy-to-letter) or property purchases in run-down areas. Lower-priced properties escape stamp duty; the problem is that governments don't have a fixed idea of what lower-priced means.

Besides stamp duty, you have legal costs, possibly a mortgage arrangement fee, a survey and, if you're letting a furnished property, an allowance for everything from curtains and chairs to cookers and cutlery. These extra expenses typically soak up £5,000 to £10,000 and represent money you can't recoup. You may also find that borrowing to fund these extra start-up costs is difficult.

Before you can think about borrowing, you need to start with how much you can put down as a deposit and how much will be soaked up by other costs. And until you know what price range you can afford, you can't go out to look at potential investment properties.

Looking at the Buy-to-Let Mortgage

Lenders will want to look at the colour of your deposit. No 100 per cent buy-to-let loans exist (and if they did, the interest rates would be prohibitive). And some lenders refuse to give mortgages on properties such as one-bedroom flats or flats above shops because they see these properties as difficult to sell if they're repossessed. If banks think these properties are tough to get rid of, take that as a hint that they are.

How much can you borrow?

Banks and building societies calculate a figure called *loan to value (LTV)*, which is the largest proportion of the property price that they'll lend you – the rest comes from you as a deposit. The LTV generally varies from 60 per cent to 85 per cent. Because you fund the balance, you need cash of between 15 per cent and 40 per cent of the property value.

If you have £20,000 to put up as a deposit, the least generous lender with a 60 per cent LTV would add £30,000, so you could buy a property costing £50,000. The lender with a high LTV (85 per cent) would convert your £20,000 into a loan of £113,333, so you could look at properties costing £133,333, or more than twice as much as the meanest lender's offering.

A higher LTV gets you a bigger property bang for your deposit bucks. But larger deposits often mean lower interest rates.

How much will you actually get?

Your deposit and the LTV set a maximum. But you may not get that amount. When you apply for a loan to buy a roof over your own head, the lender looks at the property itself to check its condition, the proportion of its value that you want to borrow and most importantly your ability to repay the debt from your salary or self-employment earnings. But because many buy-to-letters already have a mortgage banging hard against the limits of their earnings, buy-to-let lenders use a totally different way of judging how much they offer you because they see this as a business-proposition property.

Instead of looking at how much you earn, buy-to-let lenders judge how much the property will earn for you. Most banks and building societies are now involved in this market, although some specialise in buy-to-let loans.

Moneyfacts (www.moneyfacts.co.uk), an online comparison site, is a good first source of information on who's lending and their basic terms.

The simplest formula is where you tell the lender how much rent you expect each month. Suppose that amount is £500 per month, or £6,000 per year. The lender then calculates how big a loan that monthly or annual amount would back.

Suppose that interest rates stood at 6 per cent. Then your £6,000 per year would, on pure mathematics, pay back enough each month to back a £100,000 loan – irrespective of your personal income. But few lenders are stupid enough to go for that amount, especially after the 2007 credit crunch, which was caused – in part – by over-generous lending to buy-to-letters. And even though interest rates might be on the low side when the loan starts, there's no guarantee that will remain true over the 10- to 25-year life span of a typical buy-to-let mortgage.

Besides building in a safety zone against rising interest rates, there are nasty things called *voids*. These are months where you have no tenant and hence no income, or where your tenant has disappeared while owing more than the tenancy deposit. And to cap it all, there are other, unexpected, costs of ownership, such as repairs and maintenance.

Lenders insist that the rent more than covers the mortgage so you don't run on empty if something goes wrong. Typically, the rent will have to be anything from 1.3 times to 1.6 times the monthly outlay, a number called the *cover*.

Buying to let is a business proposition. So there will be risks along the way.

Buy-to-let is considered to be a commercial activity. Buy-to-let loans aren't covered by Financial Services Authority rules, which offer safeguards against misleading sales techniques aimed at mortgage customers who are buying their own home. The Financial Services Authority has shut down a number of dodgy mortgage brokers but that doesn't help to compensate victims of bad advice.

The Property Yield: A Comparison Tool

Buy-to-let isn't a magic way to make money. You need to compare its attractions against other asset classes, such as cash, bonds or shares. The easiest way is to look at the *gross yield*: what you get in rent before you spend on financing a loan. For example, take a £100,000 property rented at £500 per month. That's a £6,000 total for the year, so the yield should be 6 per cent.

But hold on. You may be spending on property-management firms like estate agents and cleaners and you'll certainly be spending on insurance. Furthermore, you run the risk of voids (months when you have no tenant). It's far better to estimate the rent on ten months per year. Now, in this example, the annual rent falls to £5,000 and so the yield drops to 5 per cent – even less when you factor in the time you'll have to spend on the property, money on maintenance and insurance, and the possibility it could take a long time (and a lot of money) to sell if you need money quickly.

Now compare that final figure with what you might get from other assets such as shares or bonds.

The future worth of your investment depends on the state of property market and the condition and location of your flat or house when you want to sell. Never forget that property values can fall as well as go up.

Property is not like a bond where the yield and capital value are closely linked in a push-pull relationship. Instead, when property prices rise, you should be able to push up the rent so you get a double benefit. But when they fall, rents tend to go down so you get a double hit.

Understanding Location, Location, Location

Why is a two-bedroom flat in Belgravia some 20 times more expensive than a similarly sized flat in Barnsley, Bolton or

Blackburn? The answer is in the property dealer's mantra of location, location, location. People pay not just for what they get but for where they get it.

Much may depend on what type of tenants you'll feel happiest with. You can provide fairly basic accommodation to students, upmarket premises to top managers from abroad on short-term UK contracts or something in between.

There's no substitute for walking around an area, sizing up the amenities, looking at estate agents and viewing properties. You can sometimes get a discount by buying *off plan*: buying from a developer who's selling units in a new or refurbished property before the building is completed (and sometimes before it's even started). In many cases, though, this discount is an illusion. Developers increase their price just so they can reduce it to convince buyers they're getting a bargain below market value. Lenders now recognise this trick, along with the fact that when a tenant moves in and the walls get scuffed, the value falls. Mortgage firms now usually base loans for new-build properties on 85 per cent of the official purchase price.

Buying off-plan can be buying blind. Don't do so just because there's an advertised incentive. In some cases the properties are never built, so you lose your deposit. This is even more true with overseas properties.

Matching tenants to the property's location

Here's how to match your preferred group with the right property type:

- ✔ **Students:** They want low-cost premises near their college or university. You may be competing with subsidised halls of residence. Expect a fair amount of cosmetic damage, supply low-cost furniture (preferably from second-hand shops) and factor in long vacations, in which case you may have no tenants. You may also have costs involved in installing fire and other safety regulations, both to satisfy the educational body and the local council. You also need to be aware of the Houses in Multiple Occupation rules, which impose extra safety standards where you let a property to five or more people.

✔ **Employed young people:** The ideal target for many land-lords. Look at areas where parking is easy and that have good employment opportunities. This group prefers to be near city centres and not stuck on a distant estate.

✔ **Families with young children:** Go for properties with gardens near schools. Public transport and access to shops can be important.

✔ **Professional high earners:** They want upscale properties and will pay for them. Many of these people will come to you through company deals, such as a firm renting your property for a long period and then installing members of its staff who need a roof over their heads.

Buying a house rather than a flat may involve costs in keeping gardens tidy, especially in void periods. You won't be popular with neighbours if you let gardens run wild. In some cases, local authorities can oblige you to keep the place in good order.

Considering properties in poor condition

Investment properties are cheap, but the term is generally a euphemism for houses and flats in poor condition. They can be profitable, however, provided that you pay for a full survey and then factor in the costs of bringing the property to a habitable condition. The period of repairs will bring in no rent but will involve outlays that you may not be able to fund through borrowing.

Here are a few additional, important points to keep in mind:

✔ You may have difficulty getting a mortgage until you get the repairs carried out.

✔ Some investment properties are in rundown areas where you'll find it hard to attract tenants, although some landlords specialise in Department of Social Security cases. You could also miss out on future property price rises as the area is unattractive and, in the worst case, face losing a lot if the property is compulsorily purchased.

Buying Overseas

Ever thought about buying an investment property in Albania, Bulgaria, Croatia or even the Cape Verde islands or Mongolia? Enterprising property developers cite these, and other locations, as the 'next big place'. But just because they say that, don't throw caution to the wind. After all, their job is to promote what they intend to build. Once they have your money, their job is over.

You can even take 'free' inspection trips where you end up seeing a field and a set of drawings, and are then persuaded to put a deposit down.

The difficulty is that while your developer is building, so too are many others. The result is over-supply and under-demand. If you want to know what happens when building gets out of control, take a look at property prices from 2005–2010 in former hot spots such as Spain and Florida.

This brings us back to location and demand. Central London, central Paris or central Manhattan property is always expensive because there isn't much of it. In places that have empty fields and not much planning control, you have to take a reality test – look at the location and demand, and the future supply, before buying property there as an investment.

Of course, if you want a second home abroad, then you're not buying an investment.

Being Aware of the Tax Issue

As far as HM Revenue & Customs is concerned, buy-to-let is a business and not an investment. You have to pay income tax on your profits from rentals, but you can deduct interest and the cost of adverts, repairs, insurance and council tax. What's left is added to your other income.

You're allowed to make a loss. And in some circumstances, losses can be carried forward against future profits. You must keep records, and many people employ an accountant (the fees can be offset against tax).

Avoiding the land scam

Wouldn't you like to invest £10,000 and turn it into £100,000 in a few years' time with no risk? Well, who wouldn't! But when it sounds too good to be true, it is. Welcome to *landbanking*, a scam that has deceived thousands.

Here's how it works. Landbankers buy a field from a farmer at £10,000 an acre. It has no planning permission. Then they call investors saying that the field is a dead cert to get the go-ahead for housing. And when that happens, the value of the land will go up 10 or even 20 times.

Each acre is divided up into 10 blocks and each block is sold for £10,000 to £15,000. So the land bought at £10,000 is sold at up to £150,000.

So far, no landbank site has ever received local authority permission to build. And given that most are just fields suitable for nothing more commercial than crops or horse grazing, none are likely to be.

Many landbanking firms have disappeared, leaving investors with a worthless piece of land that they can't even use to park a caravan or pitch a tent. But more landbankers still sell their dodgy deals.

If, or when, you sell, you'll be liable for capital gains tax on any profit, although you can deduct your annual capital gains tax allowance if you've not used it elsewhere. In some circumstances, you can deduct losses.

As you can set the mortgage interest (but not repayment of the loan itself) against tax, many buy-to-letters go for interest-only mortgages to maximise the tax relief. Interest-only mortgages are also cheaper, which makes a bigger loan more affordable.

You have to voluntarily tell HMRC that you're engaged in buy-to-let within three months of starting. The tax people won't accept excuses such as 'I was waiting for a tax form' or 'I didn't know I had to declare this'.

Investing in Commercial Property

Commercial property, such as offices, factories, warehouses and retail premises, was a lower-risk investment with a good return until the 2008 crash.

Commercial-property ownership is generally structured so that you need a minimum £50 million to £100 million to be considered a player – and even more to get a really diversified portfolio. However, some commercial-property investment opportunities exist for those whose fortunes lack most of the zeroes of the standard sums in this investment area, usually via a specialist collective vehicle.

What's good about commercial property?

In a nutshell, here are the long-term benefits of commercial property:

- ✓ Rental yields are up with higher-risk corporate bonds but with less likelihood of financial problems.
- ✓ Rents tend to increase; some properties have automatic increases every five years.
- ✓ Demand for top-class property remains high. Property buyers like the term 'primary', which can be used for a location or the quality of the building, although the two often go together because you tend to put up the best buildings on the most attractive sites.
- ✓ Overseas investors like the solidity of UK property.
- ✓ Property values tend to at least keep up with inflation.

What's bad about commercial property?

In a nutshell, here are the drawbacks of investing in commercial property:

✔ It's illiquid, so buying and selling can take ages – many property funds can lock you in for 6 or 12 months if you want to sell your holding.

✔ Returns are very susceptible to interest rates. A substantial increase can wreck the best forecasts.

✔ So-called secondary properties, the rubbish that top-class tenants avoid, can be difficult to let. If you want to imagine 'secondary property', think of rundown shopping parades, decrepit factories or office blocks that no big organisation would want to be based in.

✔ Types of property can go out of fashion. Buildings can become obsolescent or subject to new, and expensive, environmental regulations.

How to invest in commercial property

You may already have some exposure to commercial property through insurance-based with-profits or managed funds. Many packaged UK investments are also likely to have a percentage of property-company shares in the portfolio. But if you want more, there are other, less bank-busting ways than going out and buying an office block or retail development.

Property-company shares

A number of property-owning companies are listed on the London Stock Exchange. Buying and selling their shares works the same as with any other quoted equity.

Some property-owning companies have enormous portfolios, but others focus on one type of property, such as office blocks or out-of-town retail parks. Bigger firms tend to concentrate on prime property, which they rent to top household-name firms. But a number of firms go for secondary properties, hoping to make more money out of cheap buildings that they rent to less-attractive tenants. Secondary property is generally more volatile.

Investors look at two factors beyond the portfolio constituents:

✔ **Dividend yield:** This is usually higher than the market average, with the highest returns coming from property firms that go for secondary properties. The normal investment rules apply. If the dividend yield is high, then the capital gains are likely to be lower for the same level of risk.

✔ **Discount:** This is the gap between the value of the property firm's underlying portfolio less borrowings and its stock-market capitalisation. The stock-market value should generally be lower than the worth of the buildings owned.

Most property companies are now officially Real Estate Investment Trusts (REITs). This gives certain tax benefits.

Property unit trusts

These are standard unit trusts offered by a small number of investment groups to those wanting a specialist fund. They're a mix of direct investments in property, property shares and cash. The minimum investment is usually £500 or £1,000. Some may be structured as insurance-based property bonds with an appeal to a number of top-rate taxpayers.

Property bonds have nothing to do with *holiday property bonds*, a form of timeshare where you can use holiday accommodation in proportion to your holding. Holiday property bonds aren't intended as a serious investment.

Chapter 16

Delving into Exotic Investments

- -

- -

*I*f you have a nervous disposition, you may want to skip this chapter. It's all about how you can literally lose not just your shirt but everything else you own. It covers the one investment opportunity in this book from which you can end up with more than *minus everything*, because not only can your investment money go down to zero, but you also can end up owing cash over and above those losses. Very financially painful!

That sounds unbelievably awful, and it can be. So why should you grit your teeth and read this chapter? Because these types of investment, which many people now call *alternatives*, are becoming more publicised. They include contracts for difference, spread bets, traded options and covered warrants, and because of their more prominent publicity nowadays, you need to know about them if only to say no to their apparent charms.

Don't confuse these types of investment with fashioned alternative investments, such as art, wine or vintage cars. These are the new style of alternatives – investments based on stock, commodity and currency markets where you go nowhere near buying the shares, metals or foreign-exchange contracts on which they're based. Note, too, that some of these deals are called *derivatives* because they're derived from real financial securities.

 All the financial schemes in this chapter are for experienced investors who can afford to make some losses. I reckon you should always stick to what you know. It's better to be safe than sorry, whatever the adverts for these products make out!

Getting into Gear for a Faster Ride

The big difference between the investments in this chapter and elsewhere in this book is *gearing*, an arrangement in which a set sum of investment money potentially works harder for you but involves greater risk. Americans, and increasingly people in the UK, refer to gearing as *leverage*. The two terms are interchangeable.

To understand gearing, look at the difference between someone on foot and a cyclist. A pedestrian may cover five kilometres in an hour. But pedalling a bike, the same person may ride 10, 15, 20 or more kilometres in an hour. The difference is due to the fact that the cyclist has gears that transform the leg movement into greater distance when their physical effort goes through the mechanism to the back wheel. And the higher the gear used, the farther the person goes. The energy expended may be the same as when walking or even less if the cyclist freewheels.

Logically, it'd be better if everyone cycled. However, bikes have disadvantages and higher risks. It's easier to fall off a bike than to fall down as a walker. The gears are great when the going is good on the flat or downhill, but life can get tough on steep, uphill climbs. You get hit worse by bad weather. And cycling has costs.

With financial gearing, you buy an alternative or derivative of a share, a share index or bond for a fraction of its price. If the value of the underlying security goes the way you want, your investment moves up very rapidly in percentage terms. Get it wrong, and you can face total wipe-out (or worse).

To help you understand the concept, consider a simple example of a winning alternative-investment scenario:

✔ **Conventional investment:** You have £1,000, and you buy 1,000 shares in a company called ABC plc at 100p each. The shares go to 110p. You sell and earn 10 per cent on your money, giving a £100 profit. Ignoring stamp duty, dealing costs and the spread between bid and offer prices, you now have £1,100, a 10 per cent gain.

✔ **Alternative investment:** Instead of buying the shares, you go for a derivative where you only put down 10 per cent of the purchase price. You now have the equivalent of £10,000 worth of shares in ABC plc for £1,000. The shares go from 100p to 110p. But instead of having 1,000 shares, which have gained 10p, you now have 10,000, so your profit is £1,000. Again ignoring costs, your £1,000 has turned into £2,000, a 100 per cent gain.

Now look at how you can lose:

✔ **Conventional investment:** Your £1,000 buys 1,000 shares in ABC plc at 100p each. The shares fall to 90p. You sell. You've lost £100 but still have £900 left. Not good news but not a total disaster, either. You could've instead held on, hoping for an eventual uplift and taken the dividends as well.

✔ **Alternative investment:** Your £1,000 buys 10,000 shares in ABC plc at 100p each. The shares fall to 90p. You've now lost 10,000 times 10p, or £1,000, so your investment is worthless. Most alternatives don't pay dividends, and they have time limits, so you can't hold on for the longer term looking for a rebound.

Now suppose that the shares fall to 80p. With all alternative products, you lose your money. But with some alternative products, such as spread betting, it gets worse.

You not only give up your £1,000 (equal to the first 10p of the loss on each share), but you also owe the spread-bet company £1,000 for the second 10p loss per share. If ABC plc suddenly goes bust and the shares are worthless, you have to pay the whole £10,000!

Optioning Your Bets

If gearing is one side of a coin, where you increase your risk and, hopefully, your reward, then the options market is the other side of the coin. Here investors try to work out what the value of a share or other asset will be over a fixed period – often three months. But first realise that at its most simple, an option is the right but not the obligation to purchase or sell something during this time.

Imagine you want to buy a piece of art but don't know whether your partner will like it and you won't be able to check this for a week. You also know that many other art fans are hoping to buy this painting. You come to an arrangement with the art dealer where you put down a £1,000 option to guarantee you'll get the first chance to buy the artwork, which is worth £20,000. If you and your partner decide against it during the week, or never get back to the dealer, you lose the £1,000. Tough, but it's better than wasting £20,000. But suppose you decide you want it. You now pay the £20,000 plus the £1,000 option money. That's more, but you have the comfort of time to make up your mind and the reassurance you'll get the painting at the price quoted. The dealer gets £1,000, and sees that as recompense for having taken the risk of being obliged to refuse someone who might have offered substantially more.

What is a stock market option?

An *option* is a promise, backed by the stock market, that you can buy or sell a set number of shares (nearly always in parcels of 1,000 shares) in a company at a fixed price between the start day and the expiry date. You can generally choose between a number of expiry dates and a number of strike prices. A *strike price* is the value the shares have to hit before your option has any value. Remember that although this promise comes from the market, it does, of course, need another investor (or investors) to be on the other side of the deal. The company whose shares are involved will know nothing of all this.

Options are available on all sorts of investments, including bonds, shares and currencies. Equity options are the best known and the most likely to be chosen by private investors. Most are called *traded options* because investors can trade them on, buying or selling during the option period. In the art market example, you might sell your £1,000 option along with its right to buy the work at £20,000 for £2,000 to another painting purchaser who reckons this is really a masterpiece and worth £30,000. The second art fan will acquire the painting for £22,000 – £2,000 to buy the option and £20,000 to the dealer. You've doubled your money – great if you've by now decided the painting wasn't your style.

Worldwide, you can choose from thousands of options. In the UK, there are traded options on nearly all the shares in the FTSE 100 index, as well as on the index itself.

Looking at the two sides of the options contract

Just as you need two to tango, you need two to create a market. In the non-financial example I use in the introduction to this section, the two sides are the art buyer and the art dealer.

In financial options, you can divide the world between those who gear up their investments with options and those that use them to reduce risk. And you can further divide it into those who think the price of the asset will go up and those who believe it will go down.

Start with a simple *call option*, where you buy the right (but not the obligation) to buy a set number of shares in a particular company at a fixed price on or before a stated date.

This is how a call option works. You reckon the shares in ABC plc will be worth substantially more sometime over the next three months. You can buy an option to buy the shares in three months' time at 100p. The shares are now quoted at 95p – because you expect the shares to rise, you go for a strike price higher than the present quote.

You buy an option for three months at 10p on 10,000 shares for an outlay of £1,000. After the shares go past 110p (the 100p strike price for the option plus the option premium itself; you're 'in the money'). After one month, the shares stand at 120p. You then decide that's as high as they'll go, but you sell your option for 30p in the stock market to someone who believes they'll keep going up. Your profit is 10,000 times 20p, which is £2,000.

The new owner has to hope the shares will rise again. They have paid 30p for the right to buy shares in ABC plc at 100p, but only over the remaining two months. The shares have to top 130p before this buyer is 'in the money'. If the shares fall back, the option may still be worth something (but not 30p) to another investor who calculates it could be worth paying, say, 5p for the opportunity to purchase ABC plc shares at 100p.

As a rule, the longer an option has to run, the more it's worth. This is called *time value* – you may consider it as paying for more hope.

Trading Good News

The good news about options is that unlike with some of the fancy stock-market structures in this chapter, with options you can't lose more than you invest. And you can make a lot of money in a short time. The bad news? Many (probably most) option trades expire worthless. But then what do you expect from a geared investment?

The greater the potential gain, the greater the risk of losing.

You can trade options at any time before expiry. They're worthless on expiry, so the nearer you get to that date, the less valuable they become – a process called *time value*, where you pay for hope. The amount you pay for the option is called the *premium*, and it goes up with time value.

What are call prices and put prices?

Each option series for an underlying share has two sets of prices:

- ✔ **Call prices:** These prices are for investors who think the shares will go up. They give the right but not the obligation for an investor to buy the underlying shares.

- ✔ **Put prices:** These prices are for investors who think the shares will go down. They give the right but not the obligation for an investor to sell at a pre-agreed price.

A call-option example

Say that phone group BT has options that expire on a fixed date each month. You can buy up to one month ahead or for longer periods. A snapshot on one day with a stock-market price of 194p per share shows that you can choose a 180p or 200p strike price. The 180p strike price is 'in the money' for call option purchasers because the underlying shares are more valuable. The 200p strike price is 'out of the money' and has no immediate value because it's higher than the current stock-market price.

If you want to buy the call option at 180p expiring in one month's time, it costs 17.25p per share. So if the share price between now and then tops 197.25p, you have a profit.

If you think the price will go up even further, you'll do better buying the 200p strike-price series. Here, a one-month call option costs 5.5p. If BT tops 205.5p over the next month, you win. If not, your loss can't be greater than 5.5p a share.

Investors who want to take a chance on BT over longer periods pay more for their options – around 2p for an extra month.

A put-option example

If you hold the shares and want to put a floor under the price, then take out a put option. Doing so gives you the right but not the obligation to sell so you receive a set price. With the BT example, guaranteeing a right to sell in around a month at 200p costs 11p a share.

Have a look at some possibilities:

- ✔ The BT price falls to 150p. You win! You collect 200p for each share less the 11p premium. So you get 189p.

- ✔ The BT price stays unchanged at 194p. You lose. You get 200p for each share less the 11p premium. So you end up with 189p.

- ✔ The BT price soars to 250p. Your right to sell is worthless. You lose 11p per share, but some investors think this worthwhile to buy insurance-style protection. The share price might have gone the other way.

Always study how traded-option premiums move for a wide number of underlying shares before dipping your toe in this particular water. Options that have expiry dates each month rather than every three months are more heavily traded and tend to have lower dealing charges. Many strategies exist, but all involve either gearing up your investment or hedging your risk.

Strategies involving selling shares you don't own can bring limitless losses.

What is option volatility?

Winning on traded options requires having a good feel for the direction of a particular share. Will it go up or down? But you also need to know about *volatility*, the amount the shares jump around. High-volatility shares have unstable prices. The more volatile a share is, the greater the chance of the option making money but the higher the cost of the option.

You can take a bet on the volatility of the market as a whole through VIX, the Chicago Board Options Exchange's Volatility Index.

You never own the shares or other securities with traded options and other forms of derivative trading. So you have no shareholder rights. You don't get dividends either. Both those who buy and those who write options calculate the value of expected dividends.

Taking a Gamble with Spread Betting

Dyed-in-the-wool gamblers used to bet on which of two moths would hit the light bulb first and frazzle. I suppose they still do. But long gone are the days of just betting on winners in horse or dog races, or football matches, or moths on a light bulb. Nowadays, a whole new range of gambling opportunities exists (mostly opportunities to lose money, but then that's the nature of punting). There are bets on the total number of runs scored in a cricket match or the points total at rugby. Both of these bets are irrespective of which side scored them or which one wins. You can take a punt on when the first goal will be scored in a football match or the number of players sent off for foul play in a month. You can take bets on house-price moves. And you can bet on shares, bonds, currencies, stock-market indexes and other financial matters.

If there are numbers, there can be a spread bet. Whether the numbers are total points scored in a rugby match or a share price, all spread betting works in the same basic way:

1. **The bookmakers try to second-guess the most likely result.**

   Perhaps it's a total of 50 points in a rugby match or a probable price of 50p for a share in a week's time.

2. **The bookmakers create a spread either side.**

   In this case, it could be 47–53, which is called the *quote*.

3. **The punters must decide to be either long or short of the spread.**

   If they go *long*, they think that the match will be more high-scoring or the share price will be higher than the bookmakers' quotes. If they go *short*, they're thinking of a low-scoring game or a poor share price.

4. **The punters bet so much per point or penny of share price movement.**

   There might be a £10 minimum.

5. **When the match is over or the share bet reaches its expiry date, the punters look at the result.**

In this example, assume a £10 a point bet:

✔ Say that 60 points are scored at the rugby game. Those who went long win. They multiply their stake by the points over 53 to calculate their gain. So they collect £70. Those who went short lose. The bookmaker starts counting at 47, so they have to pay £130 (subtracting 47 from 60 and multiplying the resulting 13 by the £10 a point stake).

✔ Say that the result is 40. Those who shorted the bet receive £70 (£10 for each of the points between 40 and 47), and those who went long lose £130 (£10 for each of the points between 40 and 53).

✔ Say that the result is 50 – in the middle of the spread. All bets are lost, and all participants owe the bookmaker £30.

Keep in mind that you'll have to pay costs as well as deal with the spread if your bet lasts longer than one day. This is usually based on a mutually agreed interest rate. Most spread-betting websites have a section where you can take a dry run, so you can practise betting on financial assets without incurring any costs or losses.

Spread betters on financial instruments can lose limitless amounts. They may have to put up margin money each day to cover losses if they want the bet to continue to the expiry date. But punters can take profits or cut losses whenever they want. They can also reset limits one way or the other. Spread betting is leveraged, so be big gains and big losses can occur without putting up money to buy the underlying investment.

Worried that the value of your home will drop or that your dream property will soar in price well out of reach? By taking out a spread bet on the Halifax House Price Index, you can protect yourself. If you worry that property values will soar, take a spread bet on the index rising. And if you think that prices are about to plummet, take a bet on the index falling. Of course, the Halifax index is an average across the country and won't exactly replicate what's happening to the prices that concern you. And know that if you get it wrong, it could cost you more than your shirt!

Limiting Your Betting Losses with Binary Betting

The warning words *potentially unlimited losses* accompany almost everything written about spread betting and are often enough to make even those who like a flutter run a country mile.

Binary bets are different. They let you take a gamble on financial markets knowing that you can lose no more than your stake. The other side of this coin is that you also know exactly how much you could win – and it will be the same whether you're just a little or a whole lot right.

With a binary bet, you're either right or wrong. You could, for instance, bet that the stock market will be higher (or lower) at midday – or any time and any share as well as the Footsie index. You're quoted 33–36. If you think it's going up, then you bet a stake (£1, for example) at 36, costing £36. If you're right you gain £64, based on 100 less 36. If you're wrong, you lose £36. If you think it's going down, your stake is £67, based on 100 less 33. Those who are correct pick up £33, whereas losers give up £67. A quote of under 50 means that the bookmaker thinks the market will fall; over 50 implies that the market is likely to rise.

You don't pay capital gains tax on winnings from spread or binary bets. Neither can you offset your losses against capital gains tax, however.

Getting Contracts for Difference – for a Different Kind of Deal

Contracts for difference, or *CFDs* as they're known to stockmarket insiders, are a low-cost route for frequent share buyers who want a deal with, well, a difference. Instead of buying a share and holding it, the CFD investor comes to a deal with a CFD provider (usually a specialist broker) that at the end of the contract, one side or the other will pay the difference between the opening price of the contract and the closing price. Some 20 per cent of all UK equity deals are now through CFDs.

You can trade CFDs on most large UK companies, share-price indexes and many foreign companies. You can take a position in a price fall as well as hope for a rising price. And because all you're paying is the difference, you get the advantage of leverage.

At the start of the contract, you may only have to put up a small proportion of the contract value. This amount is often around 10 to 20 per cent, depending on how volatile the share is. So expect a lower percentage for a dull utility share and a higher amount for a technology stock. But because your losses could eventually exceed this margin money, brokers often insist that you deposit a minimum £10,000 before trading.

How CFDs work

Suppose that you decide shares in ABC plc look cheap at 100p and expect them to rise over the next week. You want £10,000 worth. Instead of paying dealing charges of around 1.5 per cent, plus stamp duty, plus the cost of the underlying stock, which would add up to £10,200, you go to a CFD broker. Here, you put up 10 per cent (ABC is a big company that's not volatile), and you 'borrow' the other £9,000 from the CFD provider in return for interest at a preset but variable level.

For a week, this arrangement might cost £10. You'll probably pay 0.25 per cent commission on the whole £10,000 in costs (£25). There's no stamp duty.

A week later, ABC shares can be sold for 120p, putting the value of your holding up to £12,000. You receive a £2,000 profit less £30 selling commission (that's 0.25 per cent of £12,000). Subtracting this amount plus your interest and buying costs gives a total profit of £1,935. (Note, though, that if ABC shares had gone down to 80p, your bill would've been £2,000 plus all the £65 costs.)

You can also profit if you correctly guess that a share price or an index will fall in value. This scenario is called *short trading*. Suppose that you think ABC plc is going to fall in value. If you're right, you gain. If you're wrong, you lose. It's simply the preceding example turned on its head!

The benefits and drawbacks of CFDs

Here are some plus points and drawbacks of CFDs:

✔ You can go long (expect the price to rise) or short (expect it to fall).

✔ You have a wide range of shares and indexes to choose from.

✔ Commissions are low.

✔ You leverage your stake – bigger profits but bigger losses.

✔ There's no stamp duty.

✔ You're gambling so you can forget capital gains tax or off-setting losses against capital gains elsewhere.

✔ You can hold CFDs for very short periods.

✔ They're bad value for long-term investors.

✔ You receive dividend payments where applicable.

✔ Investors who go short must pay the dividend to the broker.

✔ You may be able to place a *stop loss*, a device that automatically closes a losing position to prevent even more of your cash from bleeding away.

✔ A few brokers allow free trading.

✔ If you buy CFDs, the Financial Services Authority will consider you to be a professional and experienced investor, even if you aren't. So you can say goodbye to a large slice of your consumer protection. Beware of CFD salespeople calling you out of the blue, promising big gains for small outlays. If it was really that easy, they wouldn't be bothering to cold call you.

Don't ignore the commission and other costs, even if they sound small. CFDs are intended for short-term trading. But frequent traders face huge costs. If you have a £10,000 deposit and trade on ten times leverage (that's playing with £100,000), each buy and sell round trip will cost you 0.5 per cent of the amount you're playing with at most brokers. That's £500. If you trade just once a week for a year at this level, you end up paying your broker an amazing £26,000 plus interest (say £6,000). You've got to be really good to make money after all of this. Longer-term traders soon find the initial savings with CFDs outweighed by the running costs and the lack of dividends.

Understanding Warrants

Warrants have been around for years. They often came with investment-trust launches as a free gift for the original investors. The traditional warrant gives the right but not the obligation to buy a set number of shares in the underlying trust (sometimes in other sorts of quoted concerns) for a fixed sum during a set period each year for a number of years.

A typical launch deal might be to offer one warrant for every five shares bought at the original 100p. A £1,000 investor would get 200 warrants. These warrants then give the option to buy the underlying shares for 100p no matter what the price stands at during each September for seven years. After seven years, the warrants expire, worthless.

But warrant investors in this particular trust aren't limited to trading in September. While the warrants have value, you can buy or sell them at any time on the stock market. They're a long-term gamble on the price rising.

How about an example? Say that the warrant you received as part of an investment-trust flotation allows you to buy the actual shares for 100p in any July for the next five years. The underlying shares are worth 200p at the moment, but you want out. So another investor buys the warrant for 110p. The 10p extra is compensation for the hope value. Four years later, the shares stand at 400p. The warrant holder converts into shares. The bill is 100p, plus the 110p for the warrant, plus the interest cost of holding the warrant (there are no dividends), but the final reward is 400p. Not bad! But note that if the trust shares had slumped to 50p and stayed there, the 100p-a-time warrant money would've been wasted. Disaster!

Betting on divorces – the next big thing?

People can bet on anything, including which of two moths would burn first on a light bulb. Now a US fund manager has come up with a new idea: betting on divorce settlements. You can do this one of two ways:

✔ The less risky method is to join a fund that puts money behind divorce lawyers who work for clients who wouldn't otherwise afford their fees. Fund buyers hope that putting £50,000 of lawyer behind a divorcing person will produce more than that in alimony, or reduce the bill for the side with the money by more than £50,000. The lawyer gets a fixed fee and the fund takes a percentage of the winnings.

✔ You gamble on publicly available divorce settlement information using spread-betting techniques. You might think Celebrity A will end up with £5 million but the bookmaker is only going for a spread of £3–4 million. If you're right, you win – probably at the rate of 1p or one-tenth of 1p for every pound you're right. However, if Celebrity A ends up with nothing, you lose big time – even when the bet is for a tiny fraction of each pound!

So what's the point?

✔ Low cost

✔ No stamp duty

✔ Can be created for a sector, such as banks or pharmaceuticals

✔ No annual management fees

Part V
The Part of Tens

'Ah — here comes Mr Greystoke,
our Green Fund manager.'

In this part . . .

*T*he Part of Tens contains two vital chapters. I start
with how to deal with others – the middle people who
so often stand between you and your investment choices.
Whether they call themselves brokers, advisers or consul-
tants, they can make or break an investment strategy as
well as your savings. You don't have to listen to them. But
it's difficult to avoid them. So I offer ten tips for finding a
good adviser.

In this part's second chapter, I take a look at an even more
difficult factor in your investment life. And that's you.
Before you invest even one penny, you need to read and
apply ten helpful suggestions relating specifically to you.

Chapter 17

Ten Tips for Finding a Good Adviser

*W*hat's the point of having a financial adviser? For a growing number of investors, there's absolutely no point other than having someone to carry out transactions such as buying or selling unit trusts or shares on their behalf. Such investors have read this book, understand how investments work, know the limitations of forecasting, might like the idea of beating the so-called experts with the strategy of buying what they're selling and selling what they're buying and can carry out all their transactions online at the lowest possible cost.

But most people do like a hand to hold sometimes or a bit of help with something new. Or they simply like to seek validation or otherwise for a course of action they've worked out for themselves. Masses of people out there are willing to do these things and earn some money as a result.

You can divide investment advisers into the good, the bad and the downright ugly (just like professionals in any other field). This chapter provides ten tips for sifting out the useless and the harmful.

Know the Difference Between Tied and Independent Advisers

Financial advisers who deal with the public, as opposed to professional investors such as insurance companies and unit trusts, must show you their status under the Financial Services Act. The essential difference between these two types of professionals involves the terms *tied* and *independent*, a distinction that came into force in 1988.

Essentially, a *tied adviser* works for one investment or insurance company and can't comment on the workings or investment products from any other. An *independent financial adviser* (IFA) can discuss any investment from any firm that they want. But that doesn't mean IFAs know everything about everything. Some pretend to do so, but others wisely restrict themselves to advising on what they're really good at.

Most banks and building societies employ a tied sales force, which only promotes the often-narrow range of products on sale from that institution. These tied agency firms may carry the same name as the bank or building society – Santander or Nationwide, for example, or another brand name. So Lloyds TSB sells Scottish Widows and Barclays deals in Legal & General. Some life companies, such as Zurich or Co-operative Insurance Services, also sell all or most of their products through tied agents.

Not all tied agency firms carry the same name as the investment group whose products they sell.

Always ask tied agents what advantages they can offer to make up for the lack of variety. They'd have to promise a really good deal to get my vote.

IFAs can't claim all the moral high ground here, however. Some big firms take a radio play-list approach to investment. The top people in the firm seek out a restricted number of investment deals and push them mercilessly.

Look at Adviser Listings and Ask Questions

Why look at listings when so many advisers are screaming for your attention from the media and Internet? Because there's nothing like a local person whose office you can visit and check out. Start with your local phone directory. Look under *financial advisers.*

Financial advisers are no different from anyone else you employ to help you. You should receive an initial free consultation. Use this time to work out whether potential advisers are organised or haphazard, and whether they listen to what you want or try to impose their views on you.

Treat an adviser like a partner. Most advisers expect you to know nothing, so if you do your homework first, you'll have a good chance of getting what you want rather than their default option.

Most financial advisers like to quiz you about your life, your ambitions, your pension and, most importantly for them, how much money you may have to invest. Turn the tables on them. At the first meeting, ask as many questions about them as they ask of you. Here are some questions to ask:

- ✔ **What's your preferred customer profile?** This is a good early question because some advisers specialise in high-value clients or the elderly or taxation-linked investments.

- ✔ **How long have you been in business under your present firm's name?** Avoid someone who has changed jobs too often. Check the FSA register (www.fsa.gov.uk/register) if you have doubts.

- ✔ **How many clients do you have?** A registered individual can't really deal with more than a few hundred clients. Any more than that risks a one-size-fits-all approach.

- ✔ **Do you have a regular client newsletter?** If so, ask for back copies from the past three to five years to reflect a variety of investment scenarios.

✔ **Do you send out regular updates on my unique portfolio?** Some advisers offer a quarterly or half-yearly update that concentrates on what you have, giving an up-to-date valuation plus thoughts on your holdings with recommendations for a switch if what you've got no longer looks good.

✔ **What sort of financial problems or areas of investment do you not want to get involved with?** This is like the first question but from a different viewpoint. It's useful toward the end of the initial conversation. Advisers who say they really can't help in your circumstances should get a plaudit for honesty.

✔ **If I sign up, will I get face-to-face advice when I want it or will I have to phone a call centre?** Many advisers are now cost-cutting by reducing all but their biggest clients to a 'press one for pensions, press two for investment funds' approach.

✔ **What about regular financial check-ups?** Ask how often the adviser provides them and whether you must pay extra for them.

✔ **Are you a member of an independent financial adviser network?** If so, ask whether the network just takes care of regulatory and other paperwork or whether it dictates a list of investments. The former is preferable.

Don't forget that you should always make a final check on an adviser via the Financial Services Authority website. The site shows not just whether an adviser is registered under the regulatory regime but also whether the adviser has been disciplined.

Work Only With Advisers Who'll Negotiate Their Fees

Imagine this: a widow deposits £100,000 into her savings account after selling her home and moving somewhere smaller. The bank or building society sees this deposit and offers her a chance to improve her income. Half an hour later, she's been sold whatever the bank is pushing that month for those in her situation. The adviser may have earned as much as 7 per cent in commission. That's £7,000 for 30 minutes of easy work. Great money! And no investment risks!

Tied agents and those working for big firms rarely negotiate even if you ask. If you're happy handing out so much of your money for so little work, fine, as long as you're aware of what you're doing.

The alternative is to avoid the non-negotiators and ask for a commission-sharing scheme or pay for services by time, at a pre-agreed hourly rate, and get a 100 per cent rebate of all commission.

Also ask about *trail commission*. This is an annual amount, usually 0.5 per cent of the value of your holdings, that invest-ment-management firms give to advisers. It's supposed to pay for continuing monitoring and advice but most advisers pocket the cash. However, some will rebate half the trail if you ask. Even showing you know about trail will convince the adviser that you're not one to roll over or be rolled over.

Expect to pay a minimum £100 to £125 per hour, so always ask for an estimate of how long the job will take. It's this total that's more important than the per hour figure.

Examine the Adviser's Good and Bad Points

This tip is short and to the point: everyone talks up their good points and plays down the bad. Ask for examples of both. Take them away, study them, and then make up your mind.

Know the Difference Between Junk Mail and Real Advice

Many of the national advice firms pay a top person to natter all day on the phone to financial journalists. Doing so makes sense for them because paying for editorial mentions brings in business far more effectively than paying for adverts.

Others sponsor educational booklets with publications such as newspapers or magazines. These booklets generally offer unbiased advice of a generic nature on matters ranging from investing for income to inheritance tax.

These activities are fine, but they often lead to mailing lists, which advisers exploit to send out regular material on detailing investments that they strongly recommend. Under a controversial but gaping loophole in the Financial Services Act, such direct mailings (even when personalised with name and address) don't constitute advice but count as an advertisement on a par with a poster or a magazine advert. So, if there has been no advice, even when words such as 'I strongly recommend' appear, then logically there's no comeback from customers when they've received bad advice or been mis-sold.

The situation is quite mad. But that's the law at present. So check whether any communication you get is individual advice or not. Treat communication that's not individual advice as junk mail. It might be selling something such as dodgy penny shares that can really harm your bank balance. Recycle the mailshot, help save the planet and save your money.

Know the Adviser's Training Qualifications

All advisers, whether tied or independent, have to pass FPC3 – Financial Planning Certificate level 3 – before they can advise on anything unsupervised. FPC3 covers protection, savings and investment products; financial regulation; and identifying and satisfying client needs.

FPC3 is the equal of GCSE, a starter-level exam that's not very difficult.

Ask if the adviser has the Advanced FPC. This is the A-level exam and includes taxation and trusts, investment-portfolio management and holistic financial planning.

Advisers with advanced qualifications may not have advanced morality! These advisers might have learnt all their stuff just to rip you off better! They may use the high-level letters after their names to lead you into false confidence.

Define and Limit the Adviser's Role

Don't be afraid to delineate where you want any advice to stop. You may want to leave the basics of investment allocation up to your adviser and just take on the more interesting part, where you feel your own efforts and time will make a real difference. Or you may want to play it the other way around, asking for help with the tougher tasks.

You can't expect an adviser to take responsibility for areas where you insist on taking a do-it-yourself approach.

Determine Whether the Adviser's Adding Real Value

Is your adviser really adding value or just reading to you what's available on the Internet for free from packaged product makers – or copying that info word for word and sending it out as the advice firm's view?

Advisers obviously need a reference because no one can be expected to learn and remember all the facets of a portfolio. But the interpretation added is what makes the difference.

A good test is to see how critical the broker or adviser is of heavily advertised products. An adviser who says 'I don't know' is at least being honest and not trying to sell something doubtful.

Know Whether the Adviser Always Plays It Safe

In the past, no adviser was ever sacked for recommending IBM. But that scenario may no longer be true because Big Blue (the stock-market nickname for IBM) is no longer the be-all and end-all of computers.

Advisers who stick to the safe options are fine, but they should make it clear what they're doing. You may want to up the risk profile, and you may want something more unusual. Sometimes, today's small investment company is tomorrow's superstar. If you hope to find these shares, you've got to act now, because tomorrow will be too late.

Know Whether the Adviser Will Be There Tomorrow

It sounds daft, but you really do need to know that your adviser will be there tomorrow, and as many days as possible after that. Some firms turn their staff over every year or two.

If you find an adviser on your wavelength, cherish them and follow them to new firms when they move.

One-person businesses are supposed to set up arrangements to provide cover in the event of illness or other reasons that your adviser can't be present. Bigger firms should have their own set-ups.

To play safe, always check that the adviser is regulated by the Financial Services Authority (you can do this by going to 'Register' on the FSA website (www.fsa.gov.uk)). If you suffer as a result of a dishonest or incompetent adviser, you can ask for redress from the Financial Services Compensation Scheme (www.fscs.org.uk). But if you deal with someone – perhaps from overseas – who is not registered, you have no comeback.

Chapter 18

Ten Helpful Hints for You

*W*hen it comes to investing, you won't be 100 per cent right in what you do even if you read and inwardly digest every word of this book, or even dozens more volumes as well. But if you figure out nothing else about investment, the key lesson to remember (and here you can score maximum marks) is that it's your money, your needs (and the needs of those who depend on you) and your life that count. Losing your hard-earned savings is a cinch compared with growing them. So stop everything you're doing and don't invest a penny until you've read this chapter.

Define Where You Want to Be

Really basic questions here: what do you want from your money? Who do you want to benefit? And can you afford to lose anything? Investing isn't a game like rugby or bridge where you hope to score more than your opponents.

Always know what you want and where you're going. Don't be afraid to say that your aspirations are modest. And don't be nervous to admit that you enjoy taking a risk if you do and when you can afford to. But don't forget to put a limit on your more speculative investments.

Protect What You Have

You'll feel worse if you lose what you have than if you miss out on an investment opportunity. That safety-first option can also apply to your life and salary. Insuring the first is generally inexpensive. Buying protection against losing your earning capacity is far more expensive, but consider it if you're the breadwinner in the family.

Always check on the cover you already have from other plans and from employment before taking on more.

Pay Off the Home Loan

Most people have mortgages. Getting rid of the home loan as fast as possible is the best risk-free use you can make of spare cash because you'll save a fortune on interest payments. So do it. Ensure that paying down the home loan is at the top of your list of tasks.

Equally important, never remortgage to a larger loan to pay for an investment venture; or to buy a car; or to pay for a holiday. An investment must be consistently very clever to produce more than the interest rate on a personal loan, and such investments are very unlikely.

Accept Losses

Not all your investments will work. Full stop. Some of them will fail to gain as much as the best or even the average. Others will lose money absolutely. As an investor, you have to be tough. You have to accept that there will be days, weeks, months or even years when the signs are negative and the price screens are red with losses. Don't forget that a loss is only a loss (and a profit only a profit) when you close out the position by selling.

Don't get too worried about newspaper headlines showing one-day percentage losses. The market typically goes down in big lumps and rises in bite-sized amounts. Quality is what counts. If your investment has real potential, stick with it.

Otherwise, cut it out. Ask yourself if you can still justify the investment purchase you made.

What's really tough is the first time you accept that you've backed a real turkey and the only exit is a fast one. But it's like cutting out dead wood. You'll come out of it knowing more, feeling stronger and looking happier. Promise.

Take Your Time

Time and patience have been the great healers of investment difficulties. Or at least they have been for the past century or so, and there's no reason for a change. So time is on your side. Panic is pointless, but you can profit when others rush to sell indiscriminately. If you can keep your head when all those around you are losing theirs, you should end up well ahead.

This works the other way around too. Don't get sucked into a buying vortex unless you're very disciplined, with a clear and firm exit route.

Do the Groundwork

Are you willing to do the hard work involved with investments? This groundwork includes selecting and monitoring, and making tax returns, even if you opt for an easy portfolio building method such as picking with a pin and then holding on. You can't make gains without some pain.

If you don't want to make any effort, you can hand all your money over to a professional investment company (some will provide your tax return details as well), but there can be no guarantees that you'll get good value for your cash.

Get a Handle on the Odds

There's nothing wrong with taking bigger-than-average risks that others may consider little better than playing roulette or backing horses, provided that you're clear about what you're doing and you can afford the losses.

Don't forget that big risks really do mean slim chances of winning. Try to get a handle on the odds. The big mistake previous investors in precipice or high-income bonds (two just-about legal scams from the start of this century) made, other than taking notice of commission-chasing advisers, was that they didn't get a handle on the odds. They didn't compare the most they could gain with the most they could lose. Their top gain was a few percentage points a year more than a risk-free bank account. Their loss – and a lot lost big time – could be as much as all their investment. (Okay, the advisers didn't exactly publicise the downsides, so only those who really understood could do the calculations, and they wouldn't have been stupid enough to buy.) You wouldn't toss a coin at the start of a game if you had to call heads and there were nine tails! If there's a chance you can lose all your money, there has to be more of a chance of multiplying it many times.

Know When to Sell

Knowing when to sell is really tough. So set yourself some rules. What about selling when an investment makes a certain percentage gain or loss? Or giving it a fixed period of time? Or determining a need, such as a home improvement, family occasion or retirement, where you'll require cash and then selling when that need's time comes, no matter what?

Read the Small Print

Cigarette packets must now have a large percentage of their surface covered in health warnings. Yet no rules exist for the prominent display of wealth warnings on investments. But even if they're buried away, phrases such as 'investments can go down as well as up' mean something. Sellers and product providers will cite them as a defence if things go wrong. If you don't believe how much those who push rubbish packaged products depend on almost invisible get-out clauses, look at scandals with endowment mortgages, precipice bonds and split-level investment trusts.

Take time to read *all* the material. (Check that you have the total material and not just selected bits that some sellers try to send out.) Then ask what the worst possible scenario is.

Get it in writing. If the reality is even worse, you may have cause for compensation.

Don't get complacent just because no big scandals have hit personal money for a year or two. They never go away, and will turn up in unexpected places. And what about the big bank crash scandals? Everyone will be paying for them for years and years, one way or another.

Wake Up without Worries

The last 30 years have seen some of the most amazing financial-market manias ever. There was the collapse in the Japanese Nikkei index, which has fallen by around three-quarters since its late-1989 peak; there was the bursting of the high-tech bubble in 2000, which led to some stocks losing 99 per cent or more of their value; and, biggest of them all, the 2008–2009 bank crash, which wiped trillions (and still counting) off the world's worth. Trillions? That's 12 zeroes. And that's an awful lot of money, whether it's pounds, dollars or euros.

Your investment strategy and portfolio should allow you to go to sleep happily and to wake up without worries. Sensible investing is about not losing out to insanity. If it looks too good to be true, it probably is. No magic solutions exist. You can't defy gravity for long.

Index

FOR DUMMIES®

Making Everything Easier!™

UK editions

BUSINESS

Marketing Kit
FOR DUMMIES

978-0-470-74490-1

Business Plans Kit
FOR DUMMIES

978-0-470-74381-2

PRINCE2
FOR DUMMIES

978-0-470-71025-8

REFERENCE

British Politics
FOR DUMMIES

978-0-470-68637-9

DIY
FOR DUMMIES

978-0-470-97450-6

Researching Your Family History Online
FOR DUMMIES

978-0-470-74535-9

HOBBIES

Growing Your Own Fruit & Veg
FOR DUMMIES

978-0-470-69960-7

Allotment Gardening
FOR DUMMIES

978-0-470-68641-6

Electronics
FOR DUMMIES

978-0-470-68178-7

Anger Management
For Dummies
978-0-470-68216-6

Asperger's Syndrome
For Dummies
978-0-470-66087-4

Boosting Self-Esteem
For Dummies
978-0-470-74193-1

British Sign Language
For Dummies
978-0-470-69477-0

Cricket For Dummies
978-0-470-03454-5

Diabetes For Dummies,
3rd Edition
978-0-470-97711-8

Emotional Healing
For Dummies
978-0-470-74764-3

English Grammar
For Dummies
978-0-470-05752-0

Flirting For Dummies
978-0-470-74259-4

Football For Dummies
978-0-470-68837-3

Healthy Mind & Body All-in-One
For Dummies
978-0-470-74830-5

IBS For Dummies
978-0-470-51737-6

Improving Your Relationship
For Dummies
978-0-470-68472-6

Nutrition For Dummies,
2nd Edition
978-0-470-97276-2

Available wherever books are sold. For more information or to order direct go to www.wiley.com or call +44 (0) 1243 843291

24940 (p1)